An Intimate Portrait of
Michael Landon

by his
Eldest Daughter

I
PROMISED
MY DAD

Cheryl Landon Wilson

with Jane Scovell

SIMON & SCHUSTER

New York   London   Toronto   Sydney   Tokyo   Singapore

SIMON & SCHUSTER
Simon & Schuster Building
Rockefeller Center
1230 Avenue of the Americas
New York, New York 10020

Coypright © 1992 by Cheryl Landon Wilson

All rights reserved
including the right of reproduction
in whole or in part in any form.

SIMON & SCHUSTER and colophon are registered trademarks
of Simon & Schuster Inc.

Designed by Levavi & Levavi

Manufactured in the United States of America

1   3   5   7   9   10   8   6   4   2

Library of Congress Cataloging-in-Publication Data

Wilson, Cheryl Landon, date.
I promised my dad : an intimate portrait of Michael Landon by his eldest
daughter / Cheryl Landon Wilson with Jane Scovell.
p.   cm.
1.Landon, Michael, 1936–1991.   2.Wilson, Cheryl Landon, date.
3.Television actors and actresses—United States—Biography.
I.Scovell, Jane, date.   II.Title.
PN2287.L2814W5   1992
791.45'028'092—dc20
[B]   92-30840
CIP
ISBN 0-671-79352-7

Except where noted, all photos are from the author's collection.

To Dad, who inspired us all with his great gifts and vast love. He touched us as great men have, giving us renewed hope for ourselves and for a better world. For his family, Dad loved us, fathered us and taught us as no other could. Dad was a human angel and we will all remember him with the smiles and laughter he so deserves. This book is dedicated in loving memory to my dad . . . and to the other angel behind Dad's wings, my mother.

"Love is what lets you live on. It's the most powerful thing in the universe. Don't ever take it for granted."

—Michael Landon

Prologue

When I got home that early-April evening and found my husband, Jim, waiting for me in the doorway of our home, I knew immediately something was wrong.

I was returning from one of the regularly scheduled therapy sessions I go to each week at a clinic where I am treated for pain that continues to plague me almost twenty years after an accident that almost took my life. That pain is terrible, but it is nothing compared to the pain that awaited me that day.

"Cheryl, I have to tell you . . ." Jim began. His voice was troubled and there was a catch in his throat. A wave of panic rushed over me.

"*What?*" I cried out.

". . . someone in your family is very, very sick."

The moment he said those words, I knew who it was. Even before Jim could say his name I cried out, "Oh, no . . . not Daddy. Not my *dad!*"

Jim held me, trying to calm my hysterical crying as he told me about Dad's phone call earlier that afternoon.

Dad had asked for me.

"Hi, honey," he had said when Jim answered the phone—Dad

always called my six-foot-two-and-a-half-inch bear of a husband "honey"—"is Cheryl home?"

Jim said he thought Dad sounded different.

"No, Mike."

"Well, when do you expect her back?"

"I don't know," Jim answered, and then, sensing something wasn't right, added, "Is anything the matter?"

Jim heard Dad suck in his breath and then release it with a short gasp.

"Yeah, honey, I've got a problem. I wanted to call you guys so you'd hear it from me and not the news or the papers."

Dad paused and drew in his breath again. He spoke in measured words as though he himself didn't quite believe what he was saying. "I just came from the doctors and I have cancer in two major organs and it's inoperable."

Jim was stunned. He couldn't believe what he was hearing.

It was a few days after April 1, and for a split second, the thought crossed his mind that maybe—please, God—maybe Dad was making a joke. But, of course, Dad wouldn't do such a thing. This was no April Fool's jest; this was reality.

"Is there anything I can do, Mike?" Jim asked, struggling to keep his voice steady.

"Yes, the family is getting together tomorrow; can you come over and keep me company?" he asked.

"Of course," Jim replied.

Whenever Dad had reached out to us, we always responded. And now the whole family joined together in a combined effort to keep our dad alive, healthy and creative. For the next three months, from April to July, we stayed with him for as much time and as often as we could.

Every opportunity I was given, I stayed with Dad. Week after week, I watched as the disease took away his strength, his vitality, but it never dimmed his gallant spirit. Each day I was with him, I gained strength myself watching him face death with the same kind of courage and steadfastness with which he'd faced life.

Dad was fifty-four years old and in great condition when the cancer was discovered. He wasn't a big man but he had spent many years building up his body. He'd spent many years abusing it, too. Like most of us, Dad took his health for granted, and why shouldn't he? He'd had only one major illness in his life. He'd contracted encephalitis when he was thirty-seven and for a while his fever ran so high that it was touch and go as to whether or not he would survive. At the time the doctors told my mother that even if Dad recovered, he might suffer dramatic personality changes in the future.

But fortunately the fever broke, and Dad was back at work within a week, even though the doctors had told him to take several months off. There were no personality changes, or so it seemed at the time. Seven years later, when he left us, I wasn't the only one who wondered if this uncharacteristic behavior somehow might be related to the aftereffects of his encephalitis. True, he smoked too much, and after the divorce from Mom, drank too much as well, which he himself admitted. And his diet was overloaded with fats and junk food. Typical of Dad, he pushed himself and ignored proper nutrition. Still, he was vigorous and trim and full of life.

And now, on a balmy April evening in 1991, I learned from my husband that this invincible parent, this giant of a man, was, after all, only mortal and had been stricken with a mortal disease. I found it almost impossible to accept.

When we went to see Dad, he looked healthy. He looked strong. He looked like the man I had known and relied on since I was a little girl. Then, as each day passed, and as each of the treatments— herbs, pills, chemicals, purgatives, whatever—was tried and found ineffective, he began to fail. His great strength and indomitable will were being sapped. But what a noble fight he waged! No way was my dad leaving this life quietly, like a lamb. He was a lion, fighting for what was so very dear to him, his life . . . and his family.

So many thoughts arose during those oppressive months when we rallied around him. So many memories were revived, some good, some bad, some happy, some sad. Wounds that had torn our family apart were healed during the long days of his illness. Once again, we bonded together as a family.

Our main objective was to make him strong, to help him in his fight against this insidious cancer. All of us tried desperately to give Dad whatever he needed just so he would not leave us. I especially wanted to give back to him some of the strength he had given me.

I know this sounds impossible, yet this man, whom I fervently wished to save, had done the impossible for me. Twice he rescued

9

me from a living death, and, once, when I literally was given up for dead, he willed me back to life. Oh, how I wanted to do the same for him!

I could not.

Three months after the cancer was diagnosed, he was gone. It was so very hard at the time to accept his passing, it happened so quickly and it all seemed unreal. I still find myself unable, at moments, to believe he is dead.

This difficulty arises in part because so much of what he did is still alive. One, two, or all three of the television programs he was most closely identified with can be viewed every single day.

Here I see him in "Bonanza" as the young, handsome Little Joe finding romance and adventure on the Ponderosa. And there he is in "Little House on the Prairie" as Charles Ingalls, still handsome, still young, helping his family to carve out their place on the American prairie. Finally, there's "Highway to Heaven" and he's Jonathan Smith, the mature, handsome angel who comes to earth to help people find happiness, or, at the very least, contentment.

Just watching those programs today, I see Dad's progression as an actor-writer-director-producer. He had accomplished so much, yet there was more he wanted to do. No question, he was cut off in his creative prime. Fortunately, thanks to the medium he understood and used so brilliantly, his legacy continues.

In one sense, this book came about because of that legacy. Dad was a true American hero; his work embodies and exalts all those virtues that we as Americans are taught to hold dear. The importance of his vision for a better world, a world of strong family ties, and of honest, open affection and understanding among human beings, must not be forgotten.

Through this book I want both to remind people of what my dad stood for as an actor and a creative artist, and to celebrate my father's real-life memory, the man who was so important in my life and who lives today and every day in my memory.

For me, the television hero and the living father are inexorably tied into one. Perhaps they always were, perhaps I always saw him as a combination of the protagonists he played. Perhaps, in a way, he really was. Those fictional characters weren't "perfect," and neither was he. Yet they all, the real and the imaginary, strove for a kind of perfection, both in themselves and in the world they inhabited. Little Joe, Charles Ingalls, and Jonathan Smith had marvelous adventures. Yet none of their invented stories is any more remarkable than Dad's true story.

He came out of an abusive and wretched childhood and fashioned a worthy life for himself. He had three marriages, nine children, four grandchildren, many friends, hosts of fans, and, yes, even a few detractors. Those who esteemed him, however, far outnumber those who didn't. Yes, there were flaws in Dad's makeup, and no doubt they came out of his dismal upbringing. In my opinion, he never was fully successful in shaking off the burden of that dreadful childhood and of completely addressing his problems. To the end of his days, a part of him remained the little child desperately seeking his mother's love.

Not everyone who knew my dad will agree with my perception of who and what he was. I can only say in defense of the portrait of his life that I present that I knew him intimately. I was the eldest child in our family unit by nearly nine years. My brothers and sisters, Mark, Josh, Leslie, Michael Jr., Shawna, Christopher, Jennifer and Sean have their own versions of Dad's story; all are valid. We experience the same person in different ways and each relationship is unique. There are, however, basic elements in every one of our relationships that unite us.

Michael Landon was a part of my life for thirty years. During twenty of those years he was, without a doubt, the most significant person in my life. And during that time, I believe he was at his healthiest in mind and heart.

At his best, Dad brought his special touch to every one of his children, making every one of us feel as though we were special. He accomplished this feat with strangers as well. Anyone who has seen his shows—and I'm talking about millions and millions of people—has been affected by his vision. I cannot think of any other television performer who was able to go from one show to another and so continually and consistently hold the public's interest.

His Little Joe led to Charles Ingalls, which led in turn to Jonathan Smith. And he was working on still another series when he was taken ill. When CBS showed the pilot of Dad's project, called "Us," it earned terrific ratings. Had Dad lived, undoubtedly he would have added another name to his galaxy of enduring characters.

"Us" meant a great deal to Dad. In this story of a father who returns home after many years in prison, he planned to use the contemporary family unit to focus on current issues such as family values, education and ecology. Knowing Dad, his show would have made a difference. Viewers felt a real affinity to his characters and many followed the examples set by them. Truly, Dad was television's most durable star.

Naturally, people are curious about the man. To this day, if I am identified as "Michael Landon's daughter," the first question is, "What was he really like?" This book is an opportunity to answer that question, as far as I am able to answer it.

Besides satisfying the curiosity of others while I work out my own emotions about this very special man, there is another reason for this project.

When Dad was dying, we had many conversations. He was concerned about what would happen after he was gone. He worried especially about global issues, the ecology, the economy, education, our society and how we are destroying ourselves, all of which was reflected as themes in the "Highway to Heaven" shows. Dad had planned to continue addressing those issues in "Us." Then, as his illness progressed, his thoughts drew closer to home, and he began to concentrate on his own little world—his family.

He was greatly distressed by some of the things that happened during his illness. The awful headlines, the notoriety, the blatant prying and flagrant snooping were all upsetting. Once he became too ill to venture away from home, he was never free of the insidious whirring of a helicopter that hovered over the house. He knew what the occupants of the helicopter were after. Though security gates kept the press and curious public off the property, one of the tabloids had hired a cameraman to go up in the helicopter and try to get pictures at any angle possible. This invasion disturbed Dad almost more than anything.

"Please, honey," he asked Jim, "make sure there aren't any pictures of me. Don't let them get photographs." Jim swore he'd protect Dad's privacy. And he kept his promise.

I made a promise to my dad, too. I vowed I would protect and honor his name.

★   ★   ★

My dad had always encouraged me to write. When I was a little girl he went over my written schoolwork and would give me special assignments as well. He was a brilliant writer himself (he did most of the scripts on his shows), and had a sincere appreciation of the craft and the talent it requires.

Dad was honest in his writing. He taught me that honesty is indeed the best policy, in writing as well as in life. Therefore I will confess that even though this book was to "honor and protect" my father, in the beginning there was another component . . . anger.

At the end of his life my dad did something so out of character, so completely off-the-wall, it shocked our family. For a long time, the hurt and anger were more than I could bear. Because I could not sort out my feelings, I went on a retreat, a little while after Dad's passing. There, in a convent in Tiburon, the healing began. I learned, through guidance, that my outrage was part of my sorrow and that the power of love and forgiveness is where the journey of healing begins. Through the seminar I was able to dispel the bitterness and to work with a clear mind and conscience. In writing our story, I've been able to work out my anger and to find, if not an absolute solution, at least some reasons that can help me to understand why Dad acted as he did.

I promised my dad to protect and honor his memory. This book is my tribute to him and my way of keeping that promise. What you are about to read is as fair and factual a look at my relationship with Michael Landon as I am capable of producing.

It is an amazing story.

*M*ichael Landon came into my life when I was seven years old. He was playing Little Joe on "Bonanza" at the time, and the television Western was in its second season. Though its audience was growing, the popularity of the show had not yet reached its peak. It's hard to believe now, but in the early sixties, if you didn't watch "Bonanza," you wouldn't know who Michael Landon was.

When my mother brought me to meet her new boyfriend—she referred to him as Mike—I didn't have a clue that he was a television star. And, in fact, Mom knew only because they had met on the "Bonanza" set. He wasn't such a big deal yet, so she knew him as simply one of the actors in a Western. His great renown would come after he married my mother.

I don't recall the details of my initial meeting with my new dad. I do remember thinking Mike was "cute" and ever so friendly. He had the waviest dark hair and sparkling hazel eyes and the most wonderful smile. He also had a silly giggle, the kind of laugh that makes others laugh too. He exuded warmth and vitality. You felt good just being in his presence.

I responded to this man right away because he had something special, some quality that made him unique; it was the way he acted toward me that completely won me over. From the beginning,

Michael Landon gained my love and trust because he gave me his unconditional love and undivided attention. And I was a little girl desperately starved for both.

My parents had been divorced for as long as I could remember, and my relationship with my biological father was turbulent. At times I didn't feel comfortable with him because his temperament could turn so quickly—affectionate one minute, angry the next. I was a confused child and ached to have a loving and nurturing family environment. And then my mother met Michael Landon and my greatest dreams were realized. Here was someone who actually enjoyed being with me, who played with me and seemed to anticipate my needs. Long before he assumed the role of Charles Ingalls, television's father figure, he became a real father for me.

One of Dad's greatest gifts was his ability to reach people. He knew how to touch them and teach them without ever seeming preachy or pretentious. Sentimental, yes, but his sentiment was tempered with good common sense and irrepressible humor. His shows demonstrated his profound understanding of the human condition. He used those television programs to help make the world a better place. If he wasn't always able to live his personal life on the same exalted level of behavior as did his fictional characters, it wasn't for lack of trying. He may have fallen short in some areas, as most of us do, but he gave life his all.

Michael Landon was my knight in shining armor. I worshiped that man, and I wasn't alone. Many people idolized him and still do. I'm here to say that they're right in admiring him. He made a difference in the lives of millions who watched his programs and learned from them. But his personal influence on those people could not compare to the impact he had on me. He changed my life forever.

I was born in Los Angeles, California, on November 16, 1953. At the time my mother was 20, my father was 21, and my dad was 17. My biological parents met while they were attending Los Angeles City College. My father was tall, handsome, intelligent and thoroughly charming. I am told that he was the number-one campus hunk. My mother was his coed counterpart—she was blond, blue-eyed, and beautiful. She was smart and ambitious, too. Unfortunately that was where the similarities stopped.

Their backgrounds couldn't have been more different. My paternal grandparents immigrated to the United States from Bari,

Italy. My grandmother's first name was Bernice, and my grandfather's was Angelo Michael.

As was frequently the case then, my grandparents' marriage had been arranged. They were a traditional ethnic couple in just about every way, except that my grandmother was the breadwinner, a successful career person before women generally entered the work force. She was a costume designer for the movies and worked on such films as *Around the World in 80 Days, How the West Was Won*, and, later, *True Grit*. She designed street wear as well, and even had her own label. I remember being very impressed when she showed me the tab bearing her name. I remember also that she was a stunningly beautiful woman. I regret not having had the opportunity to know her fully.

My grandfather was known as Poppa. I don't know exactly what career he had. At various times, he'd owned bars and a small café and he and my grandmother owned the apartment building my parents lived in. However, when I was growing up, he seemed to be around the house a lot and may have been an original house husband. Bernice and Angelo had two children, my father, and his older sister, Kay.

My mother's family, whose background was a mixture of French, English, and German, were transplanted Southerners whose ancestors had been pioneers. Some were of considerable renown and reputedly included the likes of Captain Clark of Lewis and Clark fame and even Abraham Lincoln(!). Dignified, soft-spoken and genteel, my maternal grandparents had moved to California from Kentucky.

My mother, Marjorie Lynn Noe, was born in Louisville. Her only sibling, my uncle Robert, was born eleven years later in San Francisco.

We called my granddaddy General John, and he was one of a kind. He struggled through the depression and, with his brother, eventually founded EON (Noe spelled backward), the first company to manufacture seat belts for automobiles. General John was a self-made man, and there were lots of them in that family, people who started with little and moved right up.

General John and my grandmother, Virginia, had a wonderful marriage. At first they didn't have a lot of money because Granddaddy put everything he earned back into the business. The company prospered, and so, eventually, did my grandparents. They were happy, they had a lot in common and enjoyed their life together.

Granddaddy died in 1985, but my grandmother, Ginny Jean, survives, and she's still a fair-haired blue-eyed "Southern belle." My two sets of grandparents share something else besides me as their granddaughter. Both couples lived to celebrate their Golden Wedding anniversaries.

My parents met on the college campus, fell head over heels in love, married, and then quickly fell out of love. I was born shortly thereafter. It was a disaster. They simply couldn't afford me, and I don't think they had planned to have me. It was too early in the marriage for children.

My parents finally divorced when I was four years old. At first, I lived with my mother in an apartment, but the demands of full-time work while single were too difficult. She thought that living with my father and his parents would be better for me, so I moved into my grandparents' home on Aloha Drive. Good intentions aside, this was no paradise for me. My grandparents' household reflected the Latin temperament. Being part Italian myself, I understand the volcanic nature. We're very emotional and loving people and extremely volatile. In my grandparents' home, love was openly expressed, but there also was a lot of screaming and slapping. At that young age, I found myself in an uncomfortable environment filled with excitable strangers, and had problems with my two older cousins as well. Because I was the youngest, they were mean to me in the abusive way that children can be to each other. I was teased unmercifully and warned not to tell anyone. I became a frightened, moody child and experienced moments of great depression. I had no opportunity to express my anger. Though there were isolated happy occasions during those difficult three years, I lived in what felt like a child's nightmare on Aloha Drive. I later realized that my cousins were not the ogres I thought them. We were all victims of circumstance.

Looking back, I see the similarity between Michael Landon's past and mine. Though his childhood was far more hideous, Dad and I were both loners, forced to live in fear. For different reasons, we both missed the nurturing love of our mothers.

My mother and Dad Landon met on the set of "Bonanza." At the time, Mom had a pretty good modeling career. Modeling wasn't a steady job, though, so she added to her income by appearing occasionally as an extra in movies and television. Somehow the casting director got Mom, who was a *model* extra, mixed-up with an *acting* extra. When Mom reported to the set, she assumed she'd be appearing on something like "The Bob Cummings Show," a popular sitcom at the time in which Cummings played a fashion photographer and Ann B. Davis was his wisecracking sidekick. In the show he was usually surrounded by beautiful models who didn't have to do anything except stand there and look pretty. Imagine Mom's surprise when she found herself not in a photographer's studio wearing an evening gown or a bathing suit, but covered in calico and standing on the frontier set of a television Western.

Mom remembers that she got into the dress, but balked at putting on the huge bonnet that went with it. As she talked to the assistants, she looked across the stage and locked eyes with the handsome young actor who played the role of Little Joe.

BAROOM! According to everything I've ever been told by both my parents, it was love at first sight. Their eyes met, and, as Dad explained, he knew in that instant that he "had to have her," that this woman had to be his mate. According to Mom, she was a shade less moved, but only a shade, probably because she already had survived one "love-at-first-sight" encounter. Still, she couldn't deny the powerful pull she felt between her and this young actor.

Mom finished her "Bonanza" scene, but decided to stick around, something she ordinarily wouldn't do; it wasn't her style. It was obvious that something was happening, and she wasn't about to run away from it.

She got out of her costume, slipped into her own clothes, returned to the set, and stood on the sidelines with a friend, who'd also worked that day. Sure enough, when shooting finished, "Little Joe" ambled over and struck up a conversation.

Basically, my dad was a shy kind of guy who tried to mask his insecurity and reticence with jokes. Some people interpreted this behavior as brashness, because they didn't know he was covering up. Shy as he was, he nonetheless managed to ask Mom out for a drink, or rather to TELL her he was taking her out. They went to a nearby restaurant where Dad just stared at Mom the whole time and she gazed right back. It was the beginning of a pattern my parents followed for many years—all their friends tell stories about being with Mom and Dad and how suddenly they'd turn everything and everybody else off. They had eyes only for each other.

Dad and I used to play a little game called "the meeting of Lynn and Michael." I'd pretend to be Mom, putting on one of her fashion wigs that were so popular at the time. Then I'd suck in my cheeks, saunter across the room, tilt my head and look up starry-eyed at Dad. He laughed and laughed. Come to think of it, it probably was funny to see round-faced Cheryl pretending to be her high-cheekboned mother.

Dad himself told me, "I didn't even look at what was on the table in front of me. I couldn't eat or drink anything. I could only stare at your mother."

The passion that enveloped Mother and Dad was not only sudden, it was all-consuming, at least for Little Joe. He was so crazy about her that when they weren't together physically, he'd keep flipping the television dial from channel to channel hoping to get a glimpse of her in a cigarette commercial that was running at the time. He was truly besotted!

Dad pursued Mom relentlessly and within a week she fell absolutely in love with him. He said over and over that it was the first time he'd ever really loved someone, and the first time he felt equally loved in return. Yet everything wasn't rosy. Michael Landon was married, and although he and his wife lived separate lives, they still lived together. Mom really was bothered about this—she believes in traditional values and standards of morality. Being "the other woman" was something she couldn't accept. Once she learned that Dad wasn't legally free, she tried to ease off their relationship.

Mom once told an interviewer, "I would have married Michael a week after I met him but he was still married. So I decided to keep seeing him but to continue with my own life and see other men. I knew I loved him, but I was unsure."

Mom never gave Dad an ultimatum, but she did make it clear that she wasn't going to have a "Back Street" relationship. Dad was very conflicted. It drove him crazy to see Mom going out with other men, and he took to hanging around outside her apartment house to watch her comings and goings. Actually, he was spying on her. He'd park his green convertible across the street and do guard duty. Mom would come home with a date and see Dad waiting in the car.

To keep him at bay and avoid confrontation, she'd ask her escort in for a nightcap.

"I'd invite my date in, even if I had to run around the room for thirty minutes to keep him there," said Mom.

By this time, Mom was living alone in her own apartment. So Dad rented the apartment right above hers! Poor guy, he was torn apart emotionally. His marriage was washed up, yet he couldn't bear to walk out, even though he had fallen madly in love.

He kept up his cat-and-mouse courtship till Mom brought things to a head by accepting a modeling assignment in New York City. She left town for three weeks, and when she returned Dad was waiting for her. He'd decided to take control of his life and started divorce proceedings. Now he and mother openly saw each other.

Their attraction was fatal to his first marriage, no question. Dad repeatedly said he never really had been in love with his first wife, Dodie, and had only married her because he couldn't bear to disappoint her son, Mark. (I don't want to get ahead of my story, but the same kind of strange denial of affection would be declared nearly twenty years later.)

Dad also had a number of problems that made everything more complicated and difficult. For one thing he was overusing prescription drugs, and for another, he was drinking heavily. Dad was a workaholic and constantly pushed himself; a doctor had prescribed Miltown to ease Dad's anxiety. The trouble was, Dad got hooked on the things and was popping up to thirty pills a day. He simply couldn't stop. It's odd, of course—a "normal" person might overdose if he took twenty tablets, but because of Dad's addiction, he had built up a tolerance and could take an incredible amount without being affected.

"I was turning into a marshmallow," said Dad. "I couldn't do anything without getting a headache. It was so bad that I could hear the blood splashing inside my head. And in the morning when the alarm would go off, I couldn't sit up without getting a migraine. I would have to reach over to the nightstand, take three or four Miltowns with a glass of water, then lie there and wait for them to take effect so that I could get up and go to work."

Undeniably, Mom made a critical difference in helping Dad to overcome his drinking and drug habits. He wanted to be with her so much, he spent all his free time with her. Dad often said that if he hadn't met Mom, he would have developed a serious drinking problem. In all honesty, I can't say that Dad didn't have a problem. True, he eased off, but he remained a hard drinker all his life. I must add, however, that I never saw him act drunk when I was growing up.

As for the prescription drugs he was overusing, Mom gave him the strength and support necessary to enable him to quit. He went cold turkey, and to my knowledge never used them again until he contracted cancer.

The relationship between them became more and more intense. It was about this time that I first met Michael Landon, and although I cannot pinpoint the actual meeting, as I said, I do remember liking him immediately. But then, who wouldn't like him! He was such a fun person to be with. He always seemed to enjoy himself, and that infectious laugh of his was always at the ready. And toward me he was always so openly affectionate. He hugged me and comforted me and made me feel I was special. And I loved especially the fact that Mike, this grown-up, took the time to play with me! His laughter and good spirits broke the gloom on Aloha Drive like nothing else.

Mike also loved to bring me things, especially comic books. He would get down on the floor with me and read them aloud. All those cartoon adventures were made so dazzlingly real for me as we acted them out together.

He always had a present for me and I could see he took as much pleasure in giving me things as I did in receiving them. Dad took a boyish joy in getting gifts himself and had his own special way of reacting. He'd rarely open a present right away but preferred to guess at the contents. Depending on its size, he'd hold the package in front of him and turn it over and over in his hands. Then he'd put it up to his ear and shake it a little. He'd be grinning from ear to ear as he tried to guess what was in the box, and he usually identified not only the gift but also its color.

Early on he gave me a very special present, one I still have, one I will never part with. Dad bought a clown doll with this ridiculous cigar in his mouth. I called the doll Johnny, and wrote his name across his forehead. Eventually, the letters washed off. Johnny's pretty beat-up now, but I'll never let him go. In fact, there are two dolls I've kept all these years, Johnny and a beautiful model doll that Mom gave me. I treasure them both.

When I was with Mom and Mike, everything was fun, a sharp

contrast to life on Aloha Drive. I remember being one of the least-liked kids at school. I overate to compensate for my insecurity and unhappiness and grew chubby. Often hives would break out all over my body. Yet my gruesome daily life seemed less intolerable because I could look forward to visiting with Mom and her special new friend. Mike gave me such glorious moments of sheer delight, I felt I could handle anything.

Mike's divorce became final late in 1960, and on January 12, 1961, he and Mom eloped to Mexico. They were married by a justice of the peace who barely spoke English. According to Dad, the ceremony was a comic gem.

"Do you like thees man?" "Do you like thees woman?" sputtered the magistrate. When Mom and Dad replied "Yes," the justice cried out "You're MARRIED," and slammed down his hand so hard that plaster fell from the ceiling!

Mr. and Mrs. Michael Landon returned to Los Angeles and moved into an apartment on Courtney Drive. I remained at Aloha Drive, but I'd visit with my parents often, and I could see how happy Mom and Dad were together. They were even happier when Mom became pregnant. While I was glad for Mom and Mike, it all seemed somehow incomplete; I wanted to be with them all the time, especially now that a brother or sister was on the way. I didn't know they were making plans.

One day Mom phoned me and said she and Mike were coming over to ask me something important. I couldn't wait for them to get there. I think I must have guessed what the question would be. I sat on the porch in front of the house holding my doll, Johnny, in my arms. When the car drove up, I dashed over to greet them and jumped up and down with excitement as they got out of the car.

Mike and Mom hugged me and then Mom stepped back and let Mike do the talking. He was quite tongue-tied and had the hardest time addressing me. He kept circling around talking about how much he loved Mom and how much he loved me. He was trying not to come on too strong and to smooth the way for the big question. Finally, he squatted down, put his arms on my shoulders and looked me straight in the eye.

"Will you come and live with us?" he asked.

Without a pause, I cried "YES!" This was what I had prayed for. Would I come and live with them? Was he kidding?

The day I left Aloha Drive, I sat in the back of the car holding on to Johnny. I felt a joyous rush of freedom. I kept waving my hand, calling out, "Good-bye, good-bye, I'm going to live with my mom and my new dad and I'm so happy."

I remember passing by the grammar school and thinking that I would never have to go back to that place again. I was waving good-bye to all the slapping and teasing that had made me miserable. That day, an angel came into my life and my dearest and most precious dream came true. I was eight and a half years old and about to become a princess.

My new life was just as wonderful as anything I'd ever fantasized. My mother was there, and I had a dad who went to work in the morning and came home every night to be with us. And I had a brand-new baby sister, Leslie, to play with, too.

For a while we lived happily in the Courtney Drive apartment, and then my parents bought a beautiful house in Encino, not far from the ranch where Clark Gable and Carole Lombard had lived.

When we moved into the new house, Dad and Mom took me to my room—which had been decorated in pink and white just for me. My own beautiful room! I loved that room, I loved that warm and unpretentious house; I love it to this day. Encino was our Camelot.

For a good long while, I was the happiest girl in the world, and all because I had my mother's love and the love of a dear, amazing man.

Before I go on with *our* story, I'd like to go back a bit and tell you more about this man who supported, guided, and loved me—my dad, Michael Landon.

2

I have been asked many times if Michael Landon was really like the characters he portrayed. I think the best answer is "yes." Dad was an actor, a very good one, and he had the ability to make you believe in his characters. But he also had the ability to make you believe in him, and to believe him, whatever he might say or do—and you never doubted that he believed it as well. It was a talent that he had apparently had from the beginning.

If you searched and searched, you still probably wouldn't come up with a less likely name for a Hollywood star than Eugene Maurice Orowitz. That, however, was my dad's real name. The trend these days is to keep original names, but back then everything had to be homogenized, prettified, and—especially—de-ethnicized. "Eugene Orowitz" wasn't going to be a name ever at home above the title, for sure.

My dad was a complicated man and the complications were bred into him. He was born in the Forest Hills section of Queens in New York City on October 31, 1936. His parents, Eli Maurice Orowitz and Peggy O'Neill, were about as ill-matched a couple as you can imagine, and neither was cut out for marriage.

Both Dad's parents were in show business. Over his career, his father held down quite a few entertainment/theatrical jobs. He'd been a writer, but then switched to radio announcing where he appeared as Mr. Emo, on the "Lady Esther Show," which originated in New York City. He was the head of RKO Radio Pictures' East Coast publicity department for a while, and also acted as personal publicist for some pretty big stars, including the singing cowboy, Gene Autry.

When Eli met and began dating Peggy O'Neill, she was a Broadway show girl. She was quite beautiful, and no doubt he was dazzled by her looks. And so Peggy and Eli got married. Unfortunately, they had absolutely nothing in common and eventually came to loathe each other.

Dad said his mother always complained that she'd given up a great career in show business to marry a "loser" and a "nobody." She always boasted about her Broadway successes and told everyone she'd been in the Ziegfeld Follies. Well, there *was* a popular entertainer named Peggy O'Neill in the thirties, but even though Peggy Orowitz encouraged others, including her children, to believe she was that particular lady, she wasn't. My dad was mighty surprised when he discovered that his mother's tales of acclaim were pure fiction. Peggy O'Neill was a master deceiver in other ways as well. Years later, Dad found love letters from another man among his mother's possessions, all written while she was married to his father.

Dad had real problems with both his parents, particularly his mother. His older sister Evelyn was their fair-haired child, both figuratively and literally. Evelyn had inherited her mother's looks and coloring, and Peggy gave her daughter her undivided attention. That left my dad with nothing. Eli doted on Evelyn, too, and though he never was as severe or erratic in his actions toward Dad as his wife was, he wasn't supportive of him either.

Like her mother, Evelyn was very pretty. Peggy exploited her daughter's looks by pressing Evelyn into entering all sorts of local beauty pageants. Eventually, Evelyn won the title of Miss New Jersey, although that, unfortunately, was about as far as it went. You don't have to be a genius to conclude that Peggy must have been pushing her daughter to make up for her own lost career. Meanwhile, Dad was left to shift for himself. The bottom line was that throughout their childhoods Evelyn was coddled and adored, while Dad was either ignored or punished. Naturally, it tainted their relationship. While he never blamed her for the way his parents treated him, Dad never could be close to his sister. She was too much their mother's daughter. In later years, Evelyn moved into an apartment with Peggy, and Dad saw very little of them.

The Orowitzes moved to Collingswood, New Jersey, when Dad was six years old. Eli had taken a job as district manager of a theater chain. He took the steady employment only for the ensured income; in his mind, it was a comedown from his previous jobs. With the rewards of his unloved labor, Eli bought a cozy two-story brick house on a well-kept suburban street. While everything appeared normal at 623 Newall Lake Drive, Dad knew better. He lived in an armed camp and the two combatants were Eli and Peggy. Periods of screaming alternated with long stretches of utter silence.

"In my family's house," Dad once told everyone including the tabloids, "there was an incredible situation where two months could go by during which my mother and father would not speak directly to each other. It was one of those dumb things that the kid always gets stuck in the middle of.

"My mother would say, 'Tell your father dinner's ready,' and Father was only five feet away."

Though Dad remembered his family life as being pretty much near intolerable, other people, neighbors, remember a different, brighter side. To many of them, Peggy Orowitz seemed to have been a good-natured lady who sang show tunes as she cleaned the house. Kids would drop by and she'd join in with some of their games and provide refreshments. Sometimes she'd show them how to tap-dance. One neighbor called the Orowitzes "normal, average, and ordinary." Those same neighbors were shocked when, after he became famous, Dad revealed what had gone on inside the red brick house.

No question, Peggy O'Neill was mentally unstable, and her behavior correspondingly erratic. We caught glimpses of this madness many years later. Dad wouldn't give his mother our home phone number, yet she'd manage to get it from someone else. She'd call our house at odd times, often in the middle of the night. Mom took the calls to protect Dad, acting as a buffer. I never heard her raise her voice to her mother-in-law. Emotionally, Dad couldn't handle his mother; she was such a sore spot in his life. I never saw him break down except when Peggy harassed him. Invariably he'd end up crying or throwing up.

Peggy also tried to get at Dad through other members of our family. Once I was in my other grandmother's kitchen when the phone rang. Ginny Jean picked it up, said "Hello" and added, "Oh, hello, Peggy." As my grandmother listened to what was being said on the other end, tears began to run down her cheeks. I got on the phone, told Peggy to leave my grandmother alone, and hung up.

"What did that woman say to you?" I asked.

"She accused me of trying to steal her son's love away from her," said my grandmother, adding, "I'd never do anything like that."

"Of course you wouldn't," I said reassuringly. "Don't you give it another thought, Ginny Jean. She's only coming after you because she knows how wonderful you are to him and how rotten she was. Dad loves you because of who you are, not because you're competing with his mother."

Poor Dad. When he was really little, he just had to accept his mother's wanton acts of cruelty; as he grew older he learned to protect himself from her outbursts. Just about the time they moved to New Jersey, he had his birthday and Peggy informed him, "Well, now you're six and I don't like you anymore because I don't like little boys." What a stupid and thoughtless statement to make, especially to a sensitive child like Dad.

Religion was a big bone of contention in the Orowitz household. Dad said his parents grew to hate each other's faith as much as they hated each other's person. His father was a Jew who didn't like Catholics and his Catholic mother definitely despised Jews. She claimed that a priest once told her that she could not receive Holy Communion if she slept with his father. Dad calculated that they must have slept together only twice and he and Evelyn were the living proof. Peggy's anti-Semitism extended to her son. She didn't like his dark curly hair and compared it unfavorably with Evelyn's golden locks.

While Eli Orowitz wasn't a religious Jew, he did want his only son to have a bar mitzvah. In all likelihood, Eli did this less for religious reasons than to spite Peggy. As it turned out, Dad's bar mitzvah wasn't such a triumph for him, either. He went through a lot of hassle studying for the big event, which included bicycling to a nearby town every day to learn how to read the Hebrew and do the chanting. He prepared for about a year before the actual ceremony.

When the time came, he did fine. After the formal part of the bar mitzvah was over, he was chatting with relatives and friends and feeling pretty good about things when his mother drew him aside.

"I thought you'd like to know, son," she said, "that you are not Jewish. I haven't told you or anyone else, but when you were a baby, I took you out and had you baptized Catholic. This whole day has been a joke!"

As the mother of a son myself, I find it almost impossible to understand Peggy's behavior; I can only attribute it to her madness. She unrelentingly bullied everyone, including her husband. Dad felt his father shouldn't have allowed such things to happen. "He lost it, though," Dad said later, "she just wore him down."

Peggy threatened to kill herself with alarming regularity. Dad said she'd put her head in the oven more than she put in meals. He'd come home from school, smell gas, rush to the kitchen and find her on her knees in front of the stove with her head inside. After a while, Dad learned to shrug off her antics.

"I noticed," he said, "that she always had a pad under her knees so they wouldn't hurt. And the window was usually open."

One suicidal episode really stood out and my dad openly discussed it with us and the media. He was about ten and the family had taken a vacation together, a novelty in itself. They stayed in a motel on the Florida coast.

"My father had gotten up early," Dad said, "and gone to a restaurant to get fresh orange juice for my mother and sister. My sister refused to drink it, and she and my father had an argument. Then my mother went into one of her weird moods. Her eyes opened wide and she seemed to just float across the floor and out the door in her nightgown. While I was pleading with my father and sister not to argue, I looked out the window and saw my mother walking toward the water. And I knew what she was going to do, or at least try to do."

Dad dashed out of the house and followed his mother as she resolutely strode down the beach and into the surf. She didn't pay any attention to Dad, who was screaming and crying for her to stop. He stayed at her side, pulling at her arm, and soon found himself in the water. It got deeper and deeper and Dad didn't know how to swim. The water was almost over his head when he realized he had to do something or both of them would drown. He began to hit his mother in the face as hard as he could. Finally, the combination of his punches and the sudden thrust of a huge wave knocked her over.

"I pulled her onto the beach," Dad continued, "and sat on top of her while she was crying for my sister. I swear to God, forty-five minutes later my mother and sister were in their bathing suits playing in the sand as though nothing had happened. My father did nothing except to look pathetic. And I'm on the beach, at the water's edge, vomiting."

That day, Dad made a promise to himself. Never, ever would he live the way his parents did, never!

His mother's behavior continued to torment him. Dad called her "a stabber, a kicker, and a wacko," and those were the *nicer* things he could say about her. One time he was in his underwear when she came into his room wielding a knife. He was terrified she'd stab him. He tried to keep her away and at the same time protect himself. He wound up running out into the street in his skivvies.

He trembled every time he came home from school because he never knew what new terror was going to greet him. Peggy always wore her nightgown when she went on her rampages, or on those occasions when she was getting ready to "kill herself." She'd sit on the sofa holding a Bible and cry out to God to kill her and/or her son. She didn't allow Dad a moment's peace in or out of the house.

When he was about fifteen years old, he was standing in front of a drugstore talking with a few girls and boys. It was a typical teenage get-together. Suddenly a taxi pulled up and his mother jumped out. He knew immediately that trouble was coming; it was a freezing-cold day and Peggy was wearing only her nightgown. She carried a clothes hanger in her hand, and brandishing it like a hatchet, began beating him with it. While venting her fury, she turned to the girls and screamed, "Tramps! You little whores!"

Dad finally wrested the hanger away and hustled Peggy back into the cab. Trying to cover the horror with humor, he turned to the cowering girls and said, "Well, so long, time to take Mom home."

Dad spent as much time *out* of the house as possible. In summer, he'd leave before dawn and didn't come back till the sun went down. He told me he found a cave in a woods near his home and stocked it with canned goods. He'd sit in his hideaway, eating solitary meals and dreaming of the day he'd get away from the dreadful silence and/or the horrific arguments in his home. There he would imagine having his own family. His dream was that "everybody in his family would talk all the time, and be as open and affectionate as possible."

While life in the Orowitz household was hell for Dad, the world outside its confines wasn't much better. Collingswood, a typical working-class town, had only two Jewish families. Anti-Semitism prevailed. Dad said that some of the kids actually believed that Jews had horns! They'd seriously ask to feel the front of his head to see if they could find the telltale bumps. Many of the kids were just inquisitive, but some were downright nasty. Dad would be walking down the street and people passing in cars would shout "Jew bastard" out the window.

Things got even rougher when Dad reached the dating age. He remembered going to a house to pick up his date. He rang the bell and a man came to the door.

"What do you want?" the man demanded.

Dad introduced himself as Eugene Orowitz and explained that he'd come to take out the man's daughter.

"My daughter's not going out with any Jew," shouted the man, slamming the door in Dad's face.

Dad fought battles on so many fronts that it's not surprising that he underwent a big personality change when he got to high school.

As a youngster in elementary school, he'd been a model student, complete with straight A's. Quiet and polite, he was appreciated by the teachers for his sterling qualities, but not by his fellow students. He wasn't at all popular and often spent lunchtime eating alone in the school cafeteria. Dad's nickname was "Ugey." He said he'd been given the name by his sister when he was born. According to him, she thought her infant brother was homely and tried to say "ugly," only it came out "ugey." I think Dad may have been kidding. It's more likely Evelyn had trouble pronouncing Eugene. Anyway, the name stuck to him, and as he himself admitted, "Ugey" was pretty much of a nerd.

He hungered for friends, but not many sought his company. And no wonder. His own behavior was sometimes peculiar, and there was always the specter of his loony mother. It was enough to discourage fellowship.

For a while, his sorrows fed his fantasies. He retreated more and more into his solitary world. He'd take long lonely walks and dream about someday being somebody and making everyone take notice. It's hard to believe, but the future Little Joe, Charles Ingalls, and Jonathan Smith was considered to be an unattractive and scrawny youth, with ears that stuck out a mile. And as if his physique weren't enough of a problem to bear, he had a shameful physical dilemma that he tried to hide.

Dad was an enuretic, a chronic bed wetter, and he was terrified lest anyone find out. He had so few friends, and he couldn't bond with them by staying over at their homes for fear he might embarrass himself.

•Peggy went at him tooth and nail to try and get him to stop the bed-wetting. She made fun of him and called him names. When that didn't work, she took to hanging the urine-stained sheets out of the window. Now everyone would know Ugey's secret. Dad would dash home from school, run up the stairs and pull in the sheets, hoping they'd be out of sight before the other kids saw them.

The punishment and humiliation little Ugey Orowitz endured was almost inconceivable. And yet Dad was able to take these hideous experiences and use them to his advantage. In the mid-seventies, he wrote, directed, and appeared in a television movie based on his bed-wetting ordeals. *The Loneliest Runner* was shown on NBC and the off-beat story touched the hearts of millions and provided a catharsis for my dad.

His bed-wetting stopped when he was fourteen. By then, his self-esteem was "in the gutter." Dad said he felt like a "nothing person going no place." He was small, so small he used to wear padding to make himself look bigger. He'd put a sweatshirt or two under his shirt and sweatpants under his jeans to fill himself out. He remained uncommonly shy. He also developed nervous tics. He'd make gulping noises and flap his arms around. Like so many really intelligent people who get nothing for doing well in school, he decided he'd do better by not being so bright. He went from being a scholar to being a clown, and a pugnacious one at that. The repressed anger bubbled forth, and Ugey Orowitz turned from nerd to holy terror.

He picked fights with everyone and anyone. He became a real hell-raiser, fighting all the time, getting kicked out of classes, and getting lots of F's on his report card. In fact, he did so poorly at his studies, he had to repeat his sophomore year, and when he finally graduated, he was ranked 299th out of 301 students. The funny thing is, at the same time he was acting like a madman, he was developing character strengths that would aid him later on. The most important of these was his unbelievable and unstoppable sense of humor. It became his defense against all adversity.

Humor and a daredevil sense of adventure were the hallmarks of Dad's youth. He'd try anything just to get attention. Lots of kids act outrageously, but Dad brought his own brand of maniacal intensity to any situation. He became the class clown and was noted for doing foolish and often dangerous stunts. In grammar school, he dangled by his fingertips from a second-story window while his classmates and teachers looked on in horror. Another time, he jumped off the roof of a house and broke both his ankles. At the age of eleven he was playing with a friend who was seated in a swing. Dad pushed the swing and ran underneath it, turned around and pushed it back again. He began pushing and running faster and faster, and, sure enough, ran right into the swing. He wound up at the doctor's office for stitches. Dad had a penchant for splitting his flesh. Once, he got carried away while swinging a golf club. He whipped the club back in a wide arc and somehow managed to strike himself in the head.

He carried on in a similar excessive manner in the classroom. Though he had rejected the role of scholar, he amazed his high school mates by bluffing his way through assignments, particularly book reports. He never read any of the designated books but made up his own titles, authors, and plots. What's more, he got away with it. None of the teachers questioned his sources because he was so convincing.

Dad also loved to take outlandish challenges and make bizarre bets. He once bragged that he could eat fifteen hamburgers in one sitting, and when another kid challenged him and offered to pay for the burgers, Dad agreed to do it. And he did! He ate all fifteen burgers!

Besides being a cutup, Dad boasted some exceptional abilities. He could run like the wind, and used to boast that he could outrace a car. According to eyewitnesses, he'd stop kids in an automobile, point to a telephone pole about thirty yards away, and bet them two bucks he could beat them to it. And he did!

He continued his wayward ways and wacky behavior until his sophomore year. Then, in one of those fortuitous events that seem to spring from nowhere, Dad at last found something positive to do, something he could do better than anyone else.

In the late spring of his freshman year, Dad's gym class was introduced to the art of throwing the javelin. Their teacher, Maurey Dickinson, had each of the kids take a turn. Dad, the runt, was convinced he'd make a fool of himself. Still, he stepped forward and took his turn at hurling the javelin. It soared all the way across the field and into the stands, besting everyone else's throw by at least thirty feet.

Everyone stood in stunned silence, their mouths open. This was Dad's moment. He had found something he could do better than anyone else. Years later, Dad talked glowingly about that moment. He knew in an instant, this newfound talent would enable him to prove himself.

He begged the coach to let him take the javelin home for the summer so he could practice with it. Though it was against school policy, Dickinson was moved by Dad's pleas and allowed him to borrow the equipment.

That summer Dad threw the javelin, time after time after time. He put all his energy and every spare moment into perfecting his toss. He began working on throwing the shot too, and, in order to strengthen his upper body, began exercising.

Something else happened that summer, a chance event that influenced my dad for the rest of his life. He went to the movies and saw Cecil B. de Mille's biblical spectacular *Samson and Delilah*, starring Victor Mature and Hedy Lamarr. Samson's power, of course, came from his long hair, and Dad made the connection between Samson and Eugene. He decided that if he'd let his own hair grow, he'd be empowered just like the strong man of the Bible. And that's exactly what Dad did; he stopped going to the barber. As his hair grew, his javelin tosses became longer and longer.

In the tenth grade he was regional champion. In his junior year, despite a broken ankle, he came in second in the state javelin competition. And in his senior year, my dad won the state championship, a feat he accomplished by making the longest throw recorded that year in high school competition in all of the United States. He was even named all-American. He still weighed only 126 pounds, but, according to Dad, he felt as though he'd been transformed from a mouse into a lion. He was full of confidence and full of "moxie," a word Dad loved and used all the time. He wanted his kids to have moxie and I wanted to have it for him. (I had no idea where the expression "moxie" came from until it was explained to me this year. The original Moxie was a soda pop of the sarsaparilla/root-beer family. Rather than leaving you with a sweet, syrupy taste, Moxie kicked in with a strong bitter one. You really had to have guts to drink Moxie. Eventually, moxie came to mean just that—guts, backbone, courage. Moxie was the attribute my dad prized most, in himself and in others.)

With success at javelin throwing, Dad finally gained the confidence he needed. Suddenly he was being praised, and recognized for his ability and excellence. Not only that, he was offered scholarships to colleges all over the country. Everyone was impressed with the young athlete, everyone, that is, except his parents.

Dad had written his mother off long ago, and didn't expect any response from her, but he ached for his father to say something. Unfortunately, Eli didn't seem to pay any attention to his son's activities. Then, one day, Eli read in the newspaper that his son was the number-one high school javelin thrower. He didn't even know what a javelin was, but out of curiosity he went to a track meet.

Dad was excited and nervous when he saw his father at the sports field, watching him through the link fence. Dad said he threw that javelin with every ounce of strength in his body, just to show his father how good he was. Eli watched Dad compete, and then, without a word, he returned to his car and drove off. Dad was disappointed and upset. He so much wanted to please his father and make him proud. For his part, Eli just didn't seem to know what all the fuss was about.

Dad's disappointment didn't keep him from competing fiercely or from planning on a bright future. He went to work evenings at a cannery and began saving his money. His goals, naturally, were to go to college and to compete in the Olympics. For most of his high school days, furthering his education hadn't been a consideration, but his excellence at the javelin opened up the opportunity to continue his schooling. Suddenly he was a wanted man, offered scholarships from a number of schools. He carefully weighed all possibilities and opted for the University of Southern California, which had a first-rate track-and-field department.

Before he could go to USC, however, there was the little matter of graduating from high school, which wasn't going to be a piece of cake. Dad had more detention slips than anyone else. In fact, although Eugene Orowitz's javelin-throwing record was beaten some ten years after it was set, rumor has it he still holds the record for detentions at Collingswood High. The principal wouldn't let Dad get away with anything, either. He made him make up nearly three hundred hours. Dad had to sit on a bench outside Collingswood High for a month after school closed in order to receive his diploma.

Dad's impending trip to the West Coast inspired his parents to change their locale as well. Eli wanted to get out of theater managing and back into publicity. Many of the men he'd worked with in the old days were out in Hollywood with Paramount Pictures, and he was sure his former buddies would find a job for him. Peggy wanted to go west because she had decided Evelyn was going to be a movie star. The plan was for Eli and Eugene to head out first and get settled. Once the final papers had been passed on the sale of the house on Newell Lake Drive, Peggy and Evelyn would join them.

3

*I*mmediately upon his arrival at USC, Dad enrolled in the speech and drama department. He chose that area because he'd been interested in acting ever since he played a Japanese houseboy in a play presented by the Collingswood High Drama Society. Though the part had been small, the experience was significant enough that Dad later remarked on having been bitten by the acting bug at the time. It must have been just a nibble, though, because his ticket west remained the javelin and that ticket, he reckoned, might just provide passage to the Olympics. He figured that later he might be able to parlay his Olympic medals into a Hollywood career, à la previous Olympic standouts–turned–movie stars like Buster Crabbe and Johnny Weissmuller.

Dad didn't look at all like Johnny Weissmuller or Buster Crabbe; in fact, he himself said he looked more like "Supermouse." The athletic department coaches took one look at the slight, skinny youth with the mane of curly hair and threw up their hands. Could this pip-squeak be the championship javelin thrower they'd offered the scholarship to?

They lodged Dad in a fraternity house, where he was completely out of his element. Once again he was an outsider, an oddball. The contrast between him and his big, burly, crew-cut fraternity brothers was very evident. They didn't like his hair and they didn't like Eugene.

At the first practice, Dad was pitted against a giant of a guy, who towered over him. Naturally Dad beat the guy by a mile, which didn't help endear him to the giant's buddies, including all the other members of the team.

One day, about a month after he'd enrolled at USC, Dad reported for practice and, without warning, was jumped by his teammates. While several held him down, the rest clipped off the hair on one side of his head. To make their opinion of Dad even more obvious, they rubbed a muscle ointment called Atomic Balm on his scrotum.

Half-scalped, his groin burning, Dad could not defend himself. He was Ugey Orowitz once again, an outsider and helpless and alone. He had to go to a barber shop and have the rest of his hair shaved off to create a balanced crew cut. Psychologically, Dad was broken. He really believed his power, like Samson's, came from his long hair.

The next day when he went to practice, he couldn't throw the javelin well at all. Over and over, he drew back his overdeveloped left arm and hurled the spear with all his might, only to watch the javelin fall short. All he managed to do on that terrible day was tear the ligaments in his shoulder and develop an infection that eventually ended his dream of Olympic glory.

Why had his teammates turned against him? Dad thought it must have been because he was such an outsider, an Easterner who could outthrow the best man in the sports department. Maybe Dad's attitude was too smart-alecky and the others wanted to take him down a peg. Who knows? The fact is, just as he'd been the target of his grade-school classmates' gibes, he became the scapegoat for his fraternity brothers. They were out to get him and they didn't let up. A few days after his hair was shorn, he was handcuffed to the sink at the fraternity house and made to clean a huge pile of dishes while the others stood around jeering. Stupid pranks, yes, but not to Dad, whose self-esteem was too low to handle this kind of mockery.

He was humiliated by his peers and had fallen out of favor with his instructors. The athletic department was furious because he was no longer able to perform on the field.

Not surprisingly, Ugey Orowitz quit school at the end of the first semester.

To help pay the bills, he got a job loading freight cars. Once again he retreated to his dreamworld. This time he imagined how he would rebuild his shoulder muscles, enroll at UCLA, and, in his words, "kick the crap out of my ex-teammates in the javelin throw."

While Dad struggled to get along, things weren't going that well for his father either. Eli firmly believed he'd be able to resume his publicity career in Los Angeles, and before leaving New Jersey had written his former colleagues at Paramount to advise them of his arrival.

When they got to Los Angeles, Dad drove his father over to the studio. Eli told his son to pull up in front of the gate while he called in to arrange for a parking space. Eli was gone for some time. When, at last, he returned to the car, Dad immediately saw that something terrible had happened. Eli's face was drained of all color and his shoulders were stooped. Dad said he looked twenty years older than he had when he walked away.

Eli's story was not an unusual scenario for Hollywood. His former pals, now big shots, would not see him. Indeed, he couldn't even get on the lot. Eli was totally crushed and could only keep repeating, "But they were my friends. They owed me." Whatever disputes Dad had with his father, he knew the man's worth. Eli was a loyal friend who gave his all to his work, and now he'd been kicked in the face. After this experience, Eli took the first job he was offered, once again becoming a theater manager; only, this time, there was only one theater rather than a chain.

Dad made another one of his vows that day. He swore he'd never let himself get into the same position as his father. When it came to business, he'd never expect anything from anybody and he'd never owe anybody any favors, either.

Dad continued to find odd jobs. He became a baby-sitter and slept on the porch of the house where his young charges lived. Then he took a job in a soup factory and later, in a ribbon factory. Years later, he told me, "It was just ribbons, but I wanted to make the *best* ribbon." Whatever Dad did, he gave it his all. His hair had grown back, and perhaps his "powers" had, too, but he didn't test them; he'd given up all thoughts of going back to college or of making his name as an Olympic athlete. Dad had turned his full attention to acting, and, once again, it was a result more of circumstances than design.

Someone at the ribbon factory was studying acting and needed a partner to work with him on an audition scene for Warner Bros. Dad agreed to do it and was amused to see that the scene from the play, *Home of the Brave,* called for his character to do a lot of crying. Dad sobbed away. He had an uncanny ability to turn on the tears. He said he could start crying just by thinking of his childhood.

Dad liked acting and decided to pursue it as a career. Meanwhile, there were bills to pay that wouldn't wait for his career to develop. He got work pumping gas at a station right across from the Warner's lot. The proximity to the studio, Dad figured, offered a good chance for him to be discovered. His instinct proved correct. He *was* singled out by a studio executive who was impressed with Dad's looks and manner and urged him to join the acting school at Warner's.

Like most of the big studios at that time, Warner Bros. had acting classes on the lot that were open to aspiring professionals. Dad joined and for a while was in the same group as a fellow named Jim Baumgardner. Baumgardner later dropped the first syllable and the *d* of his last name and became James Garner.

Dad continued to work at his odd jobs while he studied acting. For a while he became a door-to-door blanket salesman and claimed he learned how to sell *himself* as well as the product. Most extraordinary, he became a lifeguard at a public pool. I say "extraordinary" because Dad didn't know how to swim! He talked his way into the job and apparently no one bothered to test him.

One afternoon, a child cried out for help as he went under the water, and Dad, the non-swimming lifeguard, immediately jumped into the pool. He held his breath and walked on the pool bottom. When he reached the struggling youngster, he put his arms up and pushed the boy to the surface. Then, holding his breath and bounding along, he walked the child over to the side of the pool and into the arms of his mother. The mothers applauded Dad's heroics and told him how creatively he'd saved the little fellow. They thought he'd deliberately not used the traditional neck hold. Little did they realize Dad's creativity was born out of ignorance. However, he determined it wouldn't happen again, and he spent many long hours after the pool's closing time teaching himself how to swim. Dad's method always was to take a failing or shortcoming and work to overcome it till eventually it became an attribute.

★   ★   ★

When he was nineteen, Dad met a twenty-six-year-old widow named Dodie Levy. Dodie worked as a legal secretary. Dad was drawn to her, finding her to be an understanding and warmhearted woman. Dad was particularly impressed with the way Dodie was raising her seven-year-old son Mark. She nurtured and cared for her boy, and was in every way exactly the kind of mother to Mark that Peggy never had been to Dad.

Dodie and Dad dated and fell into a relationship. They got engaged, yet Dad later admitted that he had serious doubts. Part of him wanted so to make a commitment and to be in a loving relationship, and then there was the other side of his nature, the part that drove him, that made him need to make something of himself.

Dad agonized and went to Dodie just before their wedding day and told her he didn't think it was going to work; he wanted out. Dodie, typically patient and understanding, told him it was okay with her, but that he would have to tell her son. Well, Dad simply couldn't do it. He loved Mark and wouldn't hurt him for the world. How could a man whose own childhood had been marked by rejection and desertion treat another lonely boy in the same manner? He couldn't, not if that man's name was Eugene Orowitz—or, rather, not if that man's name was Michael Landon.

Dad had changed his name. First, he'd picked "Michael Lane" out of a phone book. A Michael Lane was already a member of the Screen Actors Guild, however, and the union would allow only one. So Dad searched some more and finally settled on Michael Landon.

In 1956, Michael Landon was about to marry into a ready-made family. His mother proclaimed her displeasure and refused to attend the wedding. Dad, of course, wanted her to change her mind and stopped at his parents' place on the way to the church. His mother remained adamant and even went into one of her raving fits of anger.

"My mother pulled a knife on me," Dad later explained, "so I called the police. I told them I didn't want to hit her but I didn't want to get stabbed, either." The police came to the house. Peggy raved on about his getting married so young. One of the officers tried to calm her down and said, "Your son's of age. He can leave."

"He's mentally ill and I'm having him committed," cried Peggy, and, according to Dad, she then proceeded to call the state mental hospital. Dad left with the police. As he walked out the door he heard Peggy describing her crazy son's condition to someone at the other end of the phone.

Peggy's outburst on his wedding day was the last straw. To preserve his own sanity, he kept her at a distance from then on, never again attempting to bridge the gap that separated them. Though he remained on the outs with his mother, eventually he grew much closer to his father, especially when Eli Orowitz left his wife and moved in with Dad and Dodie. Dad always said it was too late by then for them to experience a real father-son closeness, but he did grow to appreciate what his father had gone through and had kept from him. Dad called his parents' marriage "a tragedy that never should have happened." Eli told him he'd stayed with a woman he detested only for the sake of his children. My dad seemed to have learned a lesson from his father. He wouldn't stay on with any woman just for the sake of the children.

I don't know much about Dad's first marriage, only what he'd volunteer, and he was pretty quiet about it. I do know some facts. For instance, Dad loved animals and so did Dodie and they assembled a menagerie including seven cats, two dogs, and a boa constrictor! I know also that they never had a child together. Again, Dad never said why, but since he went on to father four children with my mother and two with his third wife, I can only assume it was a conscious decision.

Dad legally adopted Mark, and later he and Dodie adopted a child named Josh. Still another infant, Jason, was adopted some time after that. Sadly, this last baby was sent back for re-adoption within a year.

It sounds so cruel: adopt a child and then return him. Who would do that? It's mystifying. All I can say is, my dad did it and yet there wasn't anyone who loved children more than Michael Landon. If I were looking for a reason, I'd say he and Dodie probably tried to pull their marriage together by bringing another child into the home. That's never a good reason to have children, however, and they found that out. I'm sure they gave Jason back believing he'd be better off having the chance to grow up in a solid family and not a broken home.

*I*n the mid-fifties, when Dad was pursuing his acting career, television drama was in its Golden Age. Virtually everything was broadcast live, and every night was like a Broadway opening. The best and the brightest were pouring their talent into the new medium. Writers like Horton Foote, Tad Mosel, Paddy Chayefsky, and Reginald Rose worked with directors like Arthur Penn, John Frankenheimer, Delbert Mann and George Roy Hill. Unknown performers like Charlton Heston, Robert Redford, Paul Newman, Jack Lemmon, Geraldine Page, and Grace Kelly started out on shows like "Playhouse 90," "Studio One," "Robert Montgomery Presents" and "Climax."

Dad appeared in bit parts on some of those shows, too. He was trying to break into the movies as well and did land a few roles in some "B" pictures. He also did stage work and got good reviews for an appearance in *Tea and Sympathy* at a West Coast playhouse.

Dad claimed he'd audition for anything, and it seems he did. He even attempted to start a singing career and went on a brief road trip with Jerry Lee Lewis, no less. He gave it all up when the tour was over because he thought his future lay in acting, not vocalizing. During his fleeting singing career, he made a recording of a song called "Gimme a Little Kiss, Will Ya, Huh?" I only heard it when

Dad performed at rodeos during his "Bonanza" days. If the record is still around, it's got to be a collector's item.

Dad didn't try singing again until decades later. In 1988 he appeared as a leather-clad punk rocker on a televised "Bob Hope Birthday Special." He was supposed to sing and dance with Brooke Shields, and while Dad could carry a tune just fine, he was a terrible dancer. He rehearsed and rehearsed and never got in step with his partner. In desperation he cried, "Let's wing it." Happily, "winging it" worked. After the show, Brooke Shields was asked what she thought of Dad. "I wish I could have been one of his children," she said.

In those early years of his first marriage, Dodie steadily provided the income while Dad steadily pursued his career.

He got his first big movie break in 1957, when he was cast in the lead role in Gene Fowler, Jr.'s *I Was a Teenage Werewolf*. With a title like that, Dad didn't expect much, but it was a starring role and he was getting paid. The strange thing is, the film has become a cult classic, and, stranger still, the scenario almost could have been written about Eugene Orowitz himself!

In the movie, Dad's character is constantly being told he's awful, like *all* teenagers. Then the adults inject him with a serum that literally turns him into the animal they've accused him of being. He's literally *forced* into being bad by society.

After *Werewolf*'s surprising success, Dad went on to play a young farmer named Dave Dawson in a screen adaptation of Erskine Caldwell's novel *God's Little Acre*. The film was called an "effective piece of Americana." (Dad's role was pretty effective, too. He played an albino, wore contact lenses, and got a terrible eye infection.) From that, he went into a minor role in *High School Confidential*, a film generally referred to as a "ghastly mishmash."

In 1959, he got the lead in another "B" film, *The Legend of Tom Dooley*, a Western inspired by the hit song by the Kingston Trio. The second week of production, Dad had his first experience with death.

Eli Orowitz usually ate lunch in a restaurant next to the theater he managed. A man of habit, he'd walk in, sit down and say, "I'll try the soup of the day." He'd take a sip and declare, "It's very good." According to Dad, he went through that routine every single day. One afternoon, Eli sipped his soup, pronounced it "good," and keeled over with a fatal heart attack. Dad told his friends that he hoped that he'd go that way, too—quick and without pain. Alas, he did not get his wish. Anyway, Dad was shocked at his response to Eli's death. He was deeply affected and genuinely grieved. Dad became convinced that he, too, would die of a heart attack, and that he would die young. Typical of Dad, he took this upsetting conviction and changed it into a kind of comedy routine in which he'd suddenly grab his chest, call out, "Adiós!" and drop to the ground. It was like Redd Foxx's TV character Sanford experiencing the "big one."

Though Peggy was around, Dad took care of Eli's funeral expenses. The fact of the matter is my dad took care of a lot of things. Once he became financially secure, he contributed to his mother's and his sister's welfare until the day he died. (Indeed, Evelyn and her daughter were included in his will.) His only stipulation was, he didn't want Peggy anywhere near him.

Dad remained shaken by his father's death even as he reported back to work on *Tom Dooley*. Later he called that movie "one of the most disastrous jobs" he ever had because of a series of mishaps that occurred during the filming.

First he accidentally stabbed himself in the face with a knife. Then blanks from a gun exploded in his face; the injury wasn't serious, but it was very painful and frightening. Then he broke his foot. The first accident, the most serious of the three, occurred when Dad was cutting through a rope with a bowie knife and didn't realize how sharp the blade was. Before he knew it, the rope had been severed and the knife was in his face. He had stabbed himself in the mouth.

Fortunately, a plastic surgeon stitched him up so that the injury didn't show. Dad used to joke about how mad some of his fellow actors were that he didn't wind up "looking like something out of Frankenstein." These guys auditioned for the same roles as Dad, and expected his face to be marred, thus removing him from competition. "They were really depressed I wasn't ruined," Dad told me.

Far from ruined, Dad had developed into one great-looking guy. Even when he was goopy Ugey, he'd had good features, except maybe for his ears, but he was so busy acting the fool, no one much noticed his looks. Now, as Michael Landon, his face had filled out and his mane of curly hair covered his ears, which had been surgically fixed. Soon, he'd become the darling of television viewers.

I think Dad always felt he was like the ugly duckling who turned into a swan. He knew he was good-looking and was very proud of it, and he worked hard to develop his physique. Mostly, though, Dad played down his looks and concentrated on his abilities.

David Dortort, a television producer, saw *Tom Dooley* and was taken with its handsome young star. He recognized Michael Landon as an actor he had seen in guest spots in TV Westerns like "The Restless Gun." Dortort needed such a fellow to join the cast of "Bonanza," a new Western he had created for NBC. Dramatic shows notwithstanding, Westerns dominated television in the late fifties; there were some *thirty* of them in prime time. Dortort wanted to present a slightly different version of the Old West, with less gunplay and more emphasis on family interaction.

The story line of "Bonanza" was straightforward. A patriarchal gentleman named Ben Cartwright had sired three sons by three different wives—all of whom had conveniently kicked the bucket. Ben and his boys, Adam, Hoss, and Little Joe, lived on the Ponderosa Ranch and had wonderful adventures. Dortort wanted a quartet of virtually unknown actors to take the principal roles. He had seen Lorne Greene on "Wagon Train," Pernell Roberts in "Cimarron City," and Dan Blocker and my dad on some guest shots on "The Restless Gun." The four were cast as father and sons.

Assuming the role of Little Joe was the turning point in Dad's career. He received five hundred dollars a week to begin with, and, of course, eventually went on to become one of the most popular and highest-paid stars in the history of television.

"Bonanza," the first color Western series, premiered on September 12, 1959. At the beginning, the odds were against the show's becoming a hit. In its initial seasons, "Bonanza" was slotted opposite "Perry Mason" on Saturday nights; more often than not, the courtroom won over boots and saddles. In the third year, the show was switched to Sunday nights and became indeed a bonanza for NBC and its stars, drawing huge audiences. In 1964, it took over the number-one spot in the Nielsen ratings, and for the next three years continued on the top of the list. In fact, the show remained in the top-ten list until two years before it ended.

Lorne Greene played the part of Ben Cartwright, Pernell Roberts was Adam, Dan Blocker was Hoss, and Dad, of course, was Little Joe. Except for Roberts, they were an exceptionally close group. Dad never did get close to "Adam," nor, for that matter, did the others. Lorne Greene, alone, remained friendly with his cantankerous "son." Consequently, no one was particularly upset when Pernell Roberts left the show in 1966, no one except, maybe, his TV father, who told him he was a damn fool. Roberts seemed to think the show was beneath his dignity, but Lorne Greene told him he should stop belly-aching and use the money he was paid to build his own theater and play all the classical roles he wanted. Roberts didn't listen and left just before the show really took off and made the rest of the Cartwrights millionaires.

Lorne Greene, by the way, was a very distinguished stage actor who'd appeared on Broadway in the company of a number of outstanding actors. He had a wonderful bass voice and a commanding presence. Dad liked and admired his TV father a lot, and he genuinely adored his giant big "brother" Hoss. Dan Blocker and Dad were alike in many ways. They both had a great sense of humor and loved to have fun, as did Blocker's children, with whom I used to play. Dad and Dan were both smart, too, although to watch the show, no one would have suspected that the young scalawag and the genial giant were extremely bright men.

"Fun" was a key word on the set of "Bonanza," and it became a part of Dad's working scheme for all his shows. For a family of seasoned cowpokes, none of the Cartwrights actually rode that tall in the saddle. Dad admitted that he wasn't much of a horseman, and said that Dan was the best, although Dad allowed as how he didn't really know if Pernell Roberts was good or not. "He didn't speak to me, so I didn't speak to him," said Dad candidly. He did know that Lorne Greene had been on a horse only once in his life prior to the show.

The opening shot of "Bonanza" showed the Cartwrights galloping toward the viewers and then coming to a halt at about a medium shot in front of the camera. Apparently, Lorne Greene was so insecure about his ability to handle his mount, he'd always cry out, "Whoa, you son of a bitch," when they drew up to the camera. Dad said it was lucky they weren't miked.

Dad was always kidding around, doing wacky things, some of them admittedly a little juvenile. If the script called for a kissing scene, he would come on the set with his jaw locked. He'd receive his instructions from the director and then take the leading lady into his arms. She'd melt toward him and he'd lean into her and open his mouth, and out from between his lips would leap a frog or a lizard or whatever small creature he'd put behind his teeth.

Dad also had a pet tarantula named Homer. He'd put Homer underneath his hat and then, during the filming, he'd lift his hat and Homer would go scurrying down his face. Lots of actresses went scurrying off the set. Playing opposite Dad really kept people on their toes.

Dan Blocker also loved jokes and pranks and frequently joined Dad in carrying them out. One time a particularly beautiful actress reported to the set. She was to play a scene with Dan and Dad in which a dog would attack her. Of course the dog was well-trained and totally harmless. Anyway, this actress didn't endear herself to the "Bonanza" bunch. She was haughty as well as pretty and spent a good long time putting down the show and letting them all know she was far superior to them and this two-bit Western she was forced to appear in. Then it came time for her scene.

She was standing with Dad and the dog was on a leash a few yards away from them. The dog was supposed to growl and attack her and she and Dad were supposed to react. Naturally, the dog was re-strained and wouldn't get anywhere near her. Dad said his lines, she said hers, and *grrrrr* went the dog. Meanwhile, Dan Blocker had come up behind the actress and at the moment the dog growled, Dan reached out and grabbed the actress's leg. She was so fright-ened she wet her pants. The snooty actress left the set thoroughly humiliated.

Dad, Lorne, and Dan made a lot of personal appearances at rodeos and parades and things like that. And the more they went around the circuit, the more popular they and their program be-came.

It was around this time that Dad met Mike North, who was to become a part of Dad's family. Mike was a press representative and had started in the business as Roy Rogers' agent, booking him into frequent appearances at state fairs and such. When Rogers retired, Mike began booking the actors from "Gunsmoke," and represented Chester, Doc, and Miss Kitty. Later, Festus took Chester's place. Then Mike was asked if he would represent Lorne Greene. Lorne brought along Dan Blocker. They did a thirty-minute act together at rodeos and were a big hit.

"It was a great 'marriage,'" said Mike, "the audiences loved seeing Ben and Hoss in person and they really didn't have to do much because rodeos were their own shows. When you booked stars, they were just frosting on the cake. You didn't have to worry about them entertaining by singing or anything like that."

Mike North was on the "Bonanza" set a lot and always said hello to Dad when he'd see him, just out of politeness. Dad was represented by another agency, a top-notch one, so Mike North was surprised when Dad's business manager called and asked him if he'd take Dad on as a client. The business manager also worked for Lorne and Dan and saw that Dad wasn't making anywhere near the money those men were. He figured out that the difference was in the extra bookings.

Dad signed with Mike North—on a handshake. A short time later, Dad called Mike from an amusement park in Oklahoma, and said, "Mike, I just want you to know I made more money this month than I made all last year with that other agency."

Dan, Dad, and Lorne began appearing together, cutting up as they often did on the set, and telling some simpleminded but good-natured jokes. A favorite topic was Dan Blocker's size, especially as compared to Dad. Blocker was six feet four and weighed close to three hundred pounds. My dad looked like a weed next to him.

One of Dad's standard lines had him saying to the crowd, "My brother Hoss loves to dance. You should see him do the twist. He looks like a runaway truck . . . and trailer."

Dad learned a lot about performing from his rodeo experiences as Little Joe, although he wasn't called upon to do much other than be that character. Then Mike North decided to vary the horse-and-cow circuit and move Dad into nightclubs. Mike told me he put Dad into a club act in Sparks, Nevada. Dad went out on stage with material that had been written by somebody else and bombed. Dad walked off the stage and went over to Mike, who was standing in the wings. Dad had tears in his eyes.

"Put me on the plane to Honolulu," he said sadly, "get me out of here."

"Mike, you got two more weeks here," answered his press representative. "You just go and do what you do best. Be yourself and play off the audience. Get them involved just like you do in the rodeos."

Dad didn't run. He did exactly what Mike told him to do. He threw out the script, worked up his own act and wowed the crowds. He became an entertainer and not just a cowboy actor. Dad always was true to himself, especially when he was performing. He wouldn't touch things that smacked of condescension or falseness. He never pandered to his audience, and if he occasionally preached, it was always with an uplifting tone and message, never a put-down.

The "Bonanza" company was like one big family, creating an atmosphere that Dad thrived in. He was one of the guys and didn't put on airs. He was the same fellow on the set as he was at home. He never needed to hang around with big stars or be in the company of big shots. He always was a man of the people.

As "Bonanza" moved up in the ratings, Michael Landon's marriage to Dodie got into trouble. It was reported that his unhappiness with his home life led to a period of pill-popping and excessive drinking that adversely affected his behavior on the set. He was still a regular guy, but occasionally he'd try to throw his weight around.

In 1962, a man named Kent McCray joined the "Bonanza" company as a production manager. McCray began his new job on location in the Santa Susana Mountains at Vasquez Rocks, a very popular place for shooting Westerns. Though it was a mere twenty minutes or so from downtown Hollywood, it looked like the middle of the plains.

The day McCray showed up was particularly hot, and Dad had been working without shade among blistering-hot rocks. He came down and was introduced to Kent McCray. "Better get a car ready for me at one o'clock," Dad told the new production manager, "because I'm leaving for the day."

Kent checked the schedule and saw that Michael Landon was supposed to be in every scene that afternoon and would have to remain on the set all day. And it was Kent McCray's duty to keep him there. Dad was in his third year as the popular Little Joe, but that didn't stop the brand-new production manager from doing his job. When my dad came over to him a second time and said, "Where's my car?" Kent answered bluntly, "There's no car and there isn't going to be one. Furthermore, it's a goddamn long walk back to Los Angeles. And if you leave before I tell you to, I'm going to sue the pants off you. You won't even get paid for your work this week—how do you like that?"

Dad's mouth hung open. "I don't like it," he answered.

"What are you going to do about it?" replied Kent, expecting the worst. Dad thought for a second and answered, "I guess I'm going back to work."

Kent knew exactly how to handle Dad, not letting himself be bullied by Michael Landon or anyone else. Dad respected his "moxie," and from that moment, they became "brothers." Their friendship continued to the very end and was expanded to include Susie Sukman, the casting director, as a "sister." She and Kent got married later on and the two of them became working partners with my dad right through "Little House," "Highway," and "Us."

The McCrays came into Dad's life about the same time as my mother, and once Mom arrived on the scene, Dad's behavior began to change for the better.

Michael Landon came of age while working on "Bonanza." He started out as an overgrown boy and by the time the show ended fourteen years later, he had become a man. And though his invented character, Little Joe, stuck close to the Ponderosa and showed no major growth in development, my dad's real character gained in stature. Give or take a few setbacks, the real person far outstripped the fictional. While Little Joe continued happy as his father's son, Michael Landon became not only his own man, but a talented, creative artist. And a good part of that development was due to the counsel and encouragement of his second wife, my mother, Lynn.

5

*B*ack in the mid-sixties, when Mom, Dad, Leslie and I moved into our new home, Encino was a small suburban town in the San Fernando Valley. The Valley once had been a resting place for Spanish explorers and Encino was named for the oak trees, or *los encinos,* which were found in the area. In the early days, the Valley was composed of giant cattle ranches and orchards. After World War II, the land was divided for suburban residential developments. These developments grew into many neighborhoods and the San Fernando Valley soon became one of the most popular and populous living areas in southern California.

When we moved there, Encino was a rural haven untouched by city life. The bustle of Los Angeles was left far behind as you drove up Ventura Boulevard toward the hills. The scent of flowers filled the air and everything was lush and green. There were open fields, and beautiful trees and wildflowers growing between the houses. The houses themselves were set apart from one another and had big backyards that went up against the hillsides. Those hillsides had yet to be landscaped with ivy, flowers, bushes, and trees; nothing was "manicured"; everything was modest and natural.

Our home, a white ranch house, was at the end of Garvin Drive. We had few neighbors; indeed, there were many empty lots on the street where wildflowers flourished alongside the great oaks. A cul-de-sac led up to a hill on which we had our driveway. We called the driveway the Fender Bender, and for a good reason. It was easy enough to drive up, but coming down, you really had to maneuver skillfully—in reverse. Big lava boulders were placed against the curves of the driveway and they could make mincemeat out of an automobile chassis. Or a little girl's knees. Once Leslie's tricycle took off like a lightning bolt and she went speeding down the driveway. Fortunately, Dad happened to be walking up to the house. Instead of slamming against the rocks, Leslie was assisted to a halt by her daddy, who magically was there to save her.

Our property was in a valley surrounded by larger hills, in a setting that was rustic and idyllic. The house was effectively hidden from all intruders, and the privacy was ideal for my family. We had few unwanted visitors, although there were certain invaders none of us would forget.

A convent of Catholic nuns was nearby; their property actually abutted ours. The nuns kept to themselves and we rarely saw them. We were, however, often visited by "members" of the convent. To provide income, the sisters raised bees and sold the honey produced by their hives. What was profitable for them was a nuisance for us.

The San Fernando Valley is well known for its scorching-hot summers. Temperatures often hover above 100 degrees. On those fiery days, swarms of bees would buzz out of the convent grounds searching for water to carry to their hives. We had a pool in our backyard and the bees would make a beeline for it. It got so bad, you couldn't be out in the yard without being pestered to death by the buzzing swarm. We went nuts trying to shoo the bees away. Dad fought back. He would get a flyswatter, climb up barefoot on the lava rocks and start smacking these pests. For every one he got, dozens more appeared, and the bottom of his feet became raw from jumping on the lava rocks. There had to be another solution. Dad couldn't spend all of his leisure time swatting bees. Finally, he and Mom went to the convent and spoke to the nuns. The result? The nuns were given a handsome sum of money to sell off their bees. They did, and everybody was happy.

A good deal of our house's charm had to do with its rustic nature. Dad in particular felt challenged by the landscape and decided to cultivate the land—himself. He didn't require much sleep, and despite the fact that he had to be on the "Bonanza" set by sunrise during the week, he never slept late, even on weekends. He was up before the crack of dawn seven days out of seven.

I never slept late either, and one morning I was at the bottom of the driveway investigating the anthills scattered around the surface. I was fascinated by the way those tiny creatures pulled together to establish their homes and provide food, and I'd put my nose to the ground watching them scamper about. I'd been at it for a while that morning when I sensed something was going on and looked up.

At the top of our hill, I saw outlined against the rising sun the figure of a man. It looked like something out of the Old West, and in a way, it was. Dad was bare-chested and wore an old pair of pants. Around his chest twined a large and cumbersome harness. The harness was attached to some sort of metal contraption in front of him. I could see Dad was having a hard time. He struggled with the cords and pushed and strained against the metal apparatus with all his might. I decided watching Dad was a lot more interesting than the ants. I abandoned the tiny hills and raced up the driveway.

"What are you doing?" I asked.

"I'm getting the earth ready for planting," Dad said, huffing and puffing. He stood there encased in the harness looking more like a galley slave than a farmer, and smiled at me. "Your mom wants roses to grow here and so they shall! And we'll get some grass for you kids to play on and some trees for shade. It's going to be beautiful, baby, just beautiful."

Dad turned back to his work. I sat and watched. It was a lesson in determination and perseverance, and in patience and love, as well.

The ground was pretty unyielding. Big rocks, huge chunks of dirt, gnarled roots and strange claylike nuggets blocked the way, yet Dad pushed and pushed. As the crude tiller inched forward, dirt and dust would fly up and back into Dad's face, coating his body. Sweat ran in rivulets down his chest and arms, matting him with grime. The soil clung to the perspiration and he began to look like some sort of prehistoric mud creature. Flying shards of rock and debris nicked his flesh until he was black and blue and bleeding from all sorts of little wounds and scrapes. Still, he kept at his chore.

All the while he labored, I watched . . . and chatted. And all the while he strained and pushed, he listened and chatted back. I'd never seen my dad so physically involved before. Many times, when he was working around the house, or writing scripts, I'd ask questions, and he'd always answer. Now, even though he was exerting incredible amounts of energy, he still took the time to respond.

I looked from the small patch of land in front of the house where Dad had started to the enormous expanse of dirt, boulders and weeds surrounding our home which were yet to be conquered. I was overcome with admiration for this man. He didn't seem in the least fazed by the magnitude of his task; he just went about doing it.

After a while, I tired of sitting in the sweltering sun and retreated to the house, where I could peek out of the window and watch Dad at work. He would pause only to come inside for an occasional drink of water. Then it was back to work.

The convent bees hadn't been bought out yet, and sure enough, as the day progressed, they buzzed into our yard. They swarmed around Dad and tried to collect some of the sweat off his body. He shook his head and paid them no mind. When I think back on that scene of Dad's struggle, it reminds me of something right out of "Little House on the Prairie."

As the sun began to set, Dad slipped out of his harness, laid down his plow and came inside. The day's work was done and now it was time to relax in the cool comfort of his air-conditioned home.

Well, theoretically, we had an air-conditioned home. There was an air conditioner which invariably broke down during heat waves. Naturally, it had conked out before Dad stopped plowing and it was warmer inside than outside the house. We had a contingency plan for just such emergencies. Whenever the air conditioner failed, we'd set up a card table in the open carport and have our dinner al fresco. That's exactly what we did that evening. The bees had retired, although there were other aggressive night creatures to contend with, like mosquitoes. We didn't care. Dining outside in the carport was one of my favorite things.

Mom was no cook. We knew it, accepted it and laughed about it. Dad, however, was a great cook and loved all foods, including the strangest culinary delights. One of his favorite bits of exotica was cooked rooster *feet*. He'd eat them with gusto and try to get us to join him. Mom couldn't bear to touch them and I can still hear her pleading, "No, Michael, please don't make me taste those things!"

★   ★   ★

After battling with the earth all day, Dad bathed and prepared our dinner. Hot days called for cold dishes and Dad rose to the occasion with a fabulous shrimp salad. I still can taste those great shrimp, crisp celery and lettuce, hard-boiled eggs and Thousand Island dressing. Mom made lemonade and iced tea. We laughed and prattled and just had fun being together.

The next day and over the course of the next several weekends, Dad worked in the yard, determined to finish the job. He met with more and more resistance; the ground just wouldn't yield. Dad knew he was fighting a losing battle with the hand tiller, so, with some reluctance, he rented a huge motorized one. After using the noisy machine for a morning and making precious little headway, Dad decided to call in a professional landscaping crew to finish the project.

Finally we had our grass lawns, a fabulous Hawaiian lava pool and waterfall, and a badminton court. Mom had her beautiful rose-bushes, too. Most important, Dad had broken the ground with his own hands to provide for his family.

During Dad's fight with cancer, I reminded him of that incident, and told him how much it had meant to me at the time to watch him at work. Dad remembered, too, and laughingly filled in a few missing details. It seems the mysterious rocks and tiles that had slammed up against his legs, leaving them black and blue, were part of the septic system. In his determination to till the soil, Dad had destroyed our sewer. He *had* to call in professionals to repair the damage. In the end, he'd paid over twenty thousand dollars to "cultivate his own land."

6

*T*here was magic in that house on Garvin Drive. I lived there from when I was eight years old until I went to college. The contrast between my life at Garvin Drive and what I had known at Aloha Drive was staggering. I couldn't believe my good fortune. Not only did I have my mother on a full-time basis, I also had the perfect father. I idolized my dad because he had rescued and transported me to a heaven on earth.

And in addition to the joy of being with my parents, I had a baby sister. Later, in 1964, Michael, Jr., was born. Then, Shawna and Christopher came along. We were the happiest family you ever could imagine.

To me, everything in Encino was perfect, but you must remember that I saw things through the eyes of, first, a child, and then, a teenager. I didn't think about the fact that Dad had an ex-wife and two other kids, Mark and Josh, and that they were growing up with their mother and without him. I barely knew about them. I only knew my dad gave his everything to me and my brothers and sisters.

Dad thought up some of the most delightful ways to keep us amused, especially on holidays. Thanksgivings and Christmases were imbued with a festive family spirit. Easter was special for me, and the time of one of my happiest childhood memories. When I was little, Dad waited till I fell asleep and then took a charcoal pencil and drew rabbit paw prints around the fireplace. I'd wake and find the telltale signs of the Easter Bunny.

When I turned thirteen, I had my first boy/girl birthday party. Dad and Mom took us all bowling and then we went for pizza. We came back to the house and danced to records. I remember that the girls danced with the girls because the boys were too shy, and just stood around talking to each other. The only mixed couple, Mom and Dad, were right in the middle of the floor dancing together and having fun. They were always involved and went all out in all our celebrations. Yes, life was sweet.

It was only when Dad left us that I realized the pain Mark and Josh must have experienced, being forced to grow up without a father. How hard this must have been on them and their mother. I still have not formally met Dodie, but I think she did a fabulous job raising her boys. Especially since she had to endure the stigma of being identified as "the woman Michael Landon married only because he loved her son." I feel there must be a lot more to her story.

Dad vowed he wouldn't stay on with any woman just for the sake of the children. And he didn't. Not with Dodie and not with my mother. I find it so tragic that Dad reacted like a frightened little boy, running away, first from Dodie and then from Mom, searching and searching.

He suffered nightmares when he was a child and they continued to plague him as a grown-up. The nightmares had to do with his parents and being poor. I think he became a workaholic partly because work was an escape from the memories that haunted him. Still, despite his intense schedule, he always made time for us. We did virtually everything together when we lived in Encino. Almost every Sunday we'd go to Barone's Restaurant for a good old-fashioned family dinner. There was constant chatter and laughter at these meals. I remember Michael, Jr., as a darling little boy. He'd sit in a high chair at the head of the table and make all sorts of funny faces. He kept us in stitches. Ginny Jean and Granddad John, and Uncle Bob were welcome participants at these dinners.

When I was twelve, old enough to take care of myself and old enough to go on occasional trips with Mom and Dad, Olive Stern came to us, Leslie and Michael's nanny. Leslie and Michael were too little to travel and Mom and Dad wanted to be sure they were well taken care of when they were on the road. Our Aunt Woo and our grandparents from Kentucky often came and stayed with us, but they needed someone steady, so they hired Olive.

Olive told me recently how she'd loved the atmosphere in our home, the close-knit family feeling. She remembered so clearly how Dad would return from work, head right for the children's room, and be with them (and me) until it was time for dinner. Often we'd play records and dance around the room together.

Dad worked hard all day, yet he never said a word about what he'd been through. If he'd had a bad day, you'd never know it. We had our evening meal together and he always had a smile on his face. He'd tune in to all of us. I swear he put himself last on the list and was constantly saying, "Come here, and tell me what I can do for you." Then he'd open his arms wide and hug you to him.

"No matter how tired he was," said Olive, "he'd always make the time to play with the children. He was such a loving man. And your mom was so lovely with you children, too. And they certainly treated me wonderfully well. Oh, and if I ever needed anything, your dad was so willing to help out.

"I belonged to an organization of English people called the Piccadilly Club. Well, they had this fund-raiser and someone found out I worked for your dad. They asked me if he would make an appearance so they could sell more tickets. I was so embarrassed to ask him. I sheepishly explained the situation and he quick as a wink says, 'Of course I'll come.'

"He did, too. It was a wonderful gesture. I mean the idea that a big star would come to such an unimportant gathering, and then take the trouble to be nice to everyone."

No question, Mom and Dad made home a very special place. I was ecstatically happy being with them and being the oldest child. At my grandparents' house, I'd been the youngest and had to take orders from my cousins. Now, I was the leader. I don't think I ever abused my "power," either. At least, I hope I didn't.

What games we played and what larks Leslie, Michael, Jr., and I had! We shared times that our younger sister and brother, Shawna and Christopher, only heard about. Basically, we were all spoiled but not spoiled rotten; we were good kids. Mom feels she spoiled me the most because she felt guilty about my early childhood. She tried to make it up with clothes and trips, and as a result I had the best wardrobe and I traveled to the best places. Dad treated me like a princess, and even though I was a half-sister to the other children in the house, I never for a minute felt like anything less than a full family member, nor was I ever treated like anything less.

In so many ways, the Landons were an ideal family. Certainly, in the beginning, before Dad made it so *big,* we were about as happy as any family could possibly be.

I, however, had something special to deal with; I had *two* families, Dad Landon's and my own father's.

As much as I was part of the Landon household, I also spent time with my biological father. At first, I wanted to. He was difficult, but he was my father and I loved him. I did everything to make him love me, too, and to understand my feelings for him.

Mom wanted me to continue the ties to my father and his family. She insisted I be brought up in the Roman Catholic Church, his faith. Well, I went to a Catholic church, and who would usually drive me to Mass? Dad Landon, of course. Eventually, I left the Church; I never felt comfortable there and I knew I was put into it only because of my mother's desire for me to remain connected to my father.

When I was around twelve, my father remarried, and for seventeen years my stepmother, Marilyn, became literally a second mother to me. Their children, Beth and Adam, are my other beloved sister and brother. Although she and my father were divorced in 1984, and she has since remarried, Marilyn remains one of my closest confidantes and best friends.

My mother wanted me to be part of my father's life, but she really didn't know the man. When I tried to tell her what he was like and how demanding it was to be with him, she would tell me to try harder. I think Mom, with her strong sense of justice, felt it was the honorable thing to do. After all, he was my father and had as much a right to their child as she.

Until I was around fourteen years old, I would visit with my father on weekends. Marilyn used to drive over and pick me up. She'd spend a few minutes talking to Mom and Dad, and then whisk me away. Sometimes those visits were fun, and sometimes they were a strain, but Marilyn always made them easier.

The atmosphere was completely different in the two households. My father didn't like the fact that I was part of another family and let me know his feelings in no uncertain terms. He put tremendous pressure on me to make choices, choices that I could not make. There was one specific directive I did follow; I had to because my father threatened to disown me if I didn't do as he said.

Once I was talking about events at the Landon house and I referred to Michael Landon as "Dad." My father hit the roof.

"Don't you ever call that man Dad. He is not your father; I'm your father!" I was too terrified to defy him. Though I wanted desperately to refer to Mike as "Dad," I honored my father's wish and called him Mike until events made it possible for me to drop the pretense and ally myself with the one man who made me feel like a beloved child.

Dad Landon never put pressure on me by making demands. He didn't try to buy affection, either. Sure, he spent lavishly on Mom and us kids as soon as he could afford to, but he gave that something else, something my own father never was able to give—unconditional love.

Dad Landon and I had an incredible emotional and spiritual bonding. He could relate to me unlike anybody else. We could look at each other and know what was in our respective thoughts. One time when I was about thirteen, we were playing a game of pool. Dad looked up and said, "Think of the number on your ball, Cheryl, and I'll tell you what it is." I wanted to trick him, so I thought of a couple of numbers, not just the one on the ball I was about to hit with the cue. Dad said quick as a flash, "Cheryl, I said *one* number!" I was taken aback. I thought of the one number and he guessed it!

Okay, maybe he'd seen the number on the ball, but I really don't think so. I honestly believe my dad had telepathic powers. Whatever it's called, he had some kind of special powers, some extra gift. That's why he was able to connect with others. You know he had a natural star on the palm of his left hand, and it was no gimmick left over from his "Teenage Werewolf" days, either.

I didn't have a star on my palm, but Dad and I did have much in common, and we'd shared so many experiences, although my background, of course, was nowhere as adverse as his had been. He empathized with what I had gone through as a child. He understood my darkness, my depressions, and my moodiness because he had all of those within himself. And because he knew me so well, I felt he loved me as no one else.

As an adult, I can understand some of my biological father's feelings. He's a proud man and he did all he could under the circumstances. Obviously, through no fault of my own, my association and devotion to Dad Landon ticked him off. He'd get furious when he'd pick up a newspaper and see a headline announcing "Michael Landon's Family," and there would be a picture of me with Dad, Mom, and the other kids. I was *his* child, not Michael Landon's.

Even though he was so possessive, the fact is my father did not contribute to the cost of my upbringing. He never handled the emotional responsibilities of a parent. He never paid child support while Mom was married to Dad, and Dad never asked him to do so. Yet he wanted to be the number-one father, which made it unbearably tough for me, especially since I never was Cheryl "Landon." The truth is, though Dad Landon wanted to adopt me legally, he couldn't; my father would not let him.

I so wanted to be able to call myself "Landon," and told Dad how I felt.

"It doesn't matter what your last name is," Dad said. "Let your name be anything, don't worry about it, it's just a name. Always remember, you're my daughter."

That's how it was with Michael Landon. He accepted me as his child even though I didn't officially bear his name.

As his child I had to abide by his rules. There weren't many. Actually, I can recall two things that Dad asked of his children. He wanted us to be first of all honest, and secondly, assertive.

"Don't ever lie to me," Dad said. "I always want to hear the truth, no matter what."

You could make mistakes, lots of them, and that was okay, so long as you owned up to your actions.

And, as hard a line as he took on lying, Dad was just as adamant about anyone acting like a "wimp." He wanted us to be strong and forceful and proud. I'm sure it had to do with his own childhood. Ugey Orowitz was classified as a "wimp," and, because of that, Michael Landon could not tolerate less than stalwart behavior from his loved ones. No wimps in his house!

Aside from those two principles—"Don't lie" and "Don't be a wimp"—we were free to do or be anything we wanted, and even when we erred, we were loved.

I never got that kind of feeling from my biological father, who is a very successful lawyer with a charismatic personality. I wanted him to know I loved him and that there was room in my heart for him as well as Dad Landon. I told my father this in person and I wrote him letters, long letters, explaining how I felt.

He refused to listen to me.

I didn't know how to deal with the problem because my father could be such fun to be with—that is, as long as Michael Landon wasn't mentioned. I attempted to be a daughter to him for years and years. Despite my efforts, and because of his jealousy, he continued to knock me down even as Dad Landon boosted me up. Dad was the one I turned to and he never spurned me. He was the one who nurtured me, unconditionally.

Dad taught me everything. He taught me how to skip rocks on the water and how to fish, his favorite sport. He was as thrilled as I was when I caught my first trout. It was Dad who was with me when I went on my first date. And it was Dad who encouraged me to do the things I most loved doing, dancing and writing.

Dad used to give me special assignments and have me write up stories for him, and then he'd go over them with me. He'd point out the good things and play down the bad. Under his guidance my imagination flourished. He'd also check my schoolwork and help with homework. It didn't matter that he was a big celebrity; he did what any good father would do.

All the years we were together, Dad never tried to step into my father's shoes; he wanted what was best for me. He was always gracious and kept himself above all the ugliness and jealousy, never tried to get at my father through me, which was exactly the opposite of my father's behavior. And, typical of Michael Landon, he'd offer himself as the target to protect me. Whenever my father would set up one of those awful demanding conditions, Dad would take me aside and say, "Look, beauty, if you have to make a choice between us, hurt me, not him." Dad knew if I crossed my father, I'd bear the brunt of his anger. That kind of situation frequently arose.

Holidays were tough. I felt as though I were in the middle of a tug-of-war. I wanted to spend those special times with my family, with my Mom and Dad and the kids. Yet I also felt obliged to be with my father and his family, and he demanded that I be there, at least until I reached my teens. I got the feeling as much as he wanted me he also wanted the "daughter who's *supposed* to be there." It made me very sad to leave my Encino haven.

One Christmas Eve, I went to my grandparents' house and there was the old cast of characters, including my aunt and her two daughters. For some reason, one of my relatives slapped one of my cousins. The cousin turned around and slapped someone else and then someone slapped someone else. Simple and silly as the whole thing was, it really set me off. I know they didn't really mean much by it, yet I couldn't help being upset by all the physical abuse. I came home in tears and went to my room. Dad came up to talk to me.

"What's bothering you, baby?" he asked.

I told him what had happened and he listened attentively. When I finished, he shook his head and burst out laughing in that wonderful infectious way of his.

"Sugar, you're looking at things the wrong way. It's not so tragic; actually, it's downright ridiculous. You've got to laugh at it. It's like a slapstick vaudeville routine. The biggest guy goes after a littler guy. Then that guy goes after a littler guy, and so on right down the line. Don't take it seriously; just laugh. Look at it as though you were an outsider."

There were many situations where I learned by example how to use a sense of humor. My Italian grandfather had lived through the Depression and was known for his frugal ways. One Sunday, Dad and Mom invited Poppa Angelo and Momma Bernice over for lunch. My parents wanted to maintain good relationships with my kin. We had a luau feast brought in from a local Chinese restaurant and set up on a buffet table. Dad watched intently as Poppa piled the food on his plate. He'd bring the overladen dish to the table, finish the contents and be up at the buffet again. Dad didn't say anything, but when the meal was over and the relatives were leaving, he handed Poppa some white boxes filled with the leftovers. Poppa was thrilled. As I watched Dad handle these sensitive situations, I could see the benefits of looking at things differently.

I took Dad's advice and tried to develop that sense of humor. My unconscious, however, wasn't as cooperative. Many nights I would cry out in my sleep and awaken from troubled dreams. When I did, Dad was always there, sitting by my bed, stroking my hair and singing softly—always the same song, "Puff, the Magic Dragon." His soothing hand and comforting voice remain a shining remembrance of my childhood.

Dad had an innate humility; he wasn't puffed up about himself. Sure, he was good-looking and increasingly popular and successful as an actor, but he wasn't a show-off. He didn't walk into a room and announce, "Here I am." Far from it. Dad was shy. Oh, he could be assertive when he had to be, but basically, he was laid back.

Sometimes, he could be caustic as well. I remember, for example, when Ed Friendly, the man who initially had the idea of bringing

"Little House" to television, got into a power struggle with Dad and accused him of trying to take over. Dad's answer was: "I know I'm perfect. It's a problem I have." In truth, Dad had a vision of the way "Little House" should be put together and it differed from Friendly's original concept. Dad prevailed, and I think the success of "Little House" proves he was right.

Dad may have given snappy answers to his peers, but he never used his biting wit on me during those key adolescent and teenage years. He was the soul of kindness. He didn't pick on "little" people and that's one of the reasons I felt so safe with him. I think "safe" is a key word in my relationship with Michael Landon. I always felt secure with him. He never failed to protect me and to assure me that things would be okay. That's why, when he left my mother, I was so taken aback and confused. Nothing in his previous behavior had prepared me for his action. But I'm getting ahead of my story.

As a child, I was subject to temper tantrums. I was very young when I pulled my first one on my dad. My mother was used to my flare-ups and adept at handling them. She was the disciplinarian. Dad didn't like to chastise his children; he preferred to be the loving, not the punishing, father. When he had to exert control, it was not through force. He did it with a look. Dad's "look" could have melted steel. Everything hardened in his face, his jaw set, his eyes narrowed and his nostrils flared. The look came rarely, and when it did, we always did as he wanted.

Sometimes Mom was just too tired to punish us and she'd use the old "wait till your father gets home" routine. Then Dad would come home and get the rundown of the transgressions and make the fair judgments.

Dad couldn't be bluffed. Davy Crockett is supposed to have said, "Be sure you're right, then go ahead," and it was a philosophy my dad followed. He wasn't *self*-righteous, just plain old righteous. He strode through my life like a true hero.

Between twelve and fourteen, I went through the awkward age, in spades! I grew to five feet seven and a half inches and despaired. I wanted to be small and cute, not tall and gawky. I really felt ugly. I used to go to my room and write morbid poems about the sadness of life. Dad would look them over and then say, "You're just going through a phase, baby. Remember, the really sought-after models are tall."

When I thought I was too tall, he made it desirable. And when I wore glasses, he made that okay too. "Intelligent people always wear glasses," he told me quite seriously. He made my nearsightedness an intellectual achievement.

When I groaned as braces were applied to my teeth, Dad laughed and said, "Relax and get ready for your future smiles."

Just before I shot up in height, I began to expand in width. Dad took me aside and talked to me. If there's anything more precarious than speaking to an adolescent girl about her weight, I don't know of it. Yet, Dad knew exactly how to handle the situation. He just said simply, "We've got to talk, honey. You know that's not baby fat anymore, so maybe you want to do something about it." The way he said it *made* me want to do something about it. It was the way he always dealt with me, reasoning, listening to my concerns. He never reacted with anger, never yelled (which was the total opposite of how I'd been raised). When I had a problem, I could just sit down with Dad and talk.

Is it any wonder that I believed my dad was perfect, better even than the character on "Father Knows Best"? He loved me when I felt ashamed and unlovable. He was understanding, kind, funny, fair . . . and, he never raised a hand to me! Wait, there actually was a time when he did.

I had just gotten to know him and I had done something wrong. I can't really recall what it was, but it was nothing big, just one of those stubborn childish acts of defiance. Maybe I said something sassy, I don't know; I only know Dad found out and confronted me.

"What's going on?" he asked.

I wouldn't answer and he repeated the question. When I kept playing dumb, he said very matter-of-factly, "You better give me an answer, or you're going to get a spanking."

I drew myself up to my fullest height, looked up at his handsome face and screamed, "If you dare to touch me, I'll tell my father and he'll beat you up."

That did it. I got the "look" and then—surprise!—Dad turned me over his knee and administered a well-deserved wallop on my rear end.

It was the first and last time my dad ever raised a hand to me, and the first and last time I tried to use my father to intimidate my dad.

7

*B*eing the child of a celebrity has built-in annoyances. The upside is swell—the special recognition, the wonderful trips, the gifts, the opportunity to meet other celebrities, all the attention heaped upon the famous which dribbles down to those who are with them. The downside is less thrilling. You have to develop a keen sense to know who truly *is* your friend, and who's interested in you just because you are the daughter of someone famous.

When you're young, there's a strange combination of wanting to tell people your parent is famous, and at the same time wanting to keep it a secret. Anyone who has gone through this experience has to understand what I mean. You're real proud, on the one hand, but on the other, sometimes you just don't want to be connected with anything or anybody other than yourself.

I attended the Lanai Road Elementary School, which was not far from our Encino house. My brothers and sisters all attended private schools at one time or another, and there is a difference. The private schools have many celebrity children, and you can't go around feeling like a big shot because your mother or father is "so-and-so" for the simple reason that the kid sitting next to you might be the child of "such-and-such."

At the Lanai Road Elementary School, there were only two "celebrity" children—I and the son of a man who did television commercials for used cars.

I was known as "Cheryl Michael-Landon's-daughter," as though the description were my last name.

Some kids befriended me for one purpose only. I remember two girls in particular who called me up for a play date. I went over to the one girl's house and the three of us had a pretty good time.

The next day, the doorbell rang at our house and there were my two new chums.

"Hi, Cheryl," they said in unison.

"Hi," I said.

The girls peered around me and looked inside. "Is your dad home?" one of them asked.

"No," I said.

"Will he be coming home soon?" inquired the other.

"No, he's working."

"Oh, well, we'll see you around," was the reply, and off they went, leaving me standing in the doorway.

You didn't have to be a rocket scientist to figure out these so-called chums were interested in me simply because they wanted to get a glimpse of Michael Landon. Needless to say, I dropped them from my roster of friends. Happily, not all kids were as obvious as those two. I made some beautiful friendships at the Lanai Road Elementary, at Portola Junior High, and later at Birmingham High. I'm still close to many of those people.

Whenever anyone heard I was Michael Landon's daughter, the first question asked was "What's he really like?" Some form of this query is directed at *everyone* who is close to a celebrity, whether it's a movie or television star, a sports figure, a dress designer, a general, a politician, or whatever. While I cannot speak for all celebrities, I can say, in basic ways, my dad was like the characters he portrayed on the screen—at least he was for me.

He came into my life when he was Little Joe. Little Joe was a teen idol. He was a ladies' man; quick to act and react. Fortunately, his big brothers and his "pa" rescued him when the going got too tough. Feisty, full of beans, and with a dazzling smile, Little Joe was the boy next door in spurs. He was totally engaging and very young—just like my dad.

Though Dad had been married and had children, in many ways he was a kid himself. A bright kid, to be sure, but still a kid. He got into scrapes on the show, and in life. He had a lot of growing up to do, and that's where Mom really helped out. According to friends, he'd been under great pressure during the last years of his first marriage. He lived beyond his means and was having money problems. He couldn't, or wouldn't, find solace at home with Dodie.

When he and Mom met, she noticed his erratic behavior right away, and then realized it was due to the hard drinking and pill-popping. She helped him deal with the problems.

I never was affected by this aspect of my dad, because in our relationship, he was the all-wise, all-caring, all-loving parent. The patches of trouble in our home weren't the sort of thing I, as a child, would have noticed. I knew nothing about his unhappiness in his first marriage. Why would I? He wasn't unhappy when he was with me and I assumed he was the same warm, wonderful guy in every situation.

I knew my dad worked very, very hard. I didn't know he had to because not only was he responsible for our upkeep, he had alimony payments to his first wife. He'd never shirk on those, either. With Mom at his side, he worked through his difficulties. Later, after Mom and he had split, Dad said he'd looked to God to give him the strength to stop using drugs. He gave absolute credit to the Almighty and conveniently forgot Mom's contribution.

It's not easy to discuss my parents' marriage in the light of what happened. Even with hindsight, I cannot see the "seams." To me and everyone who knew them, it was the most incredible union imaginable. Dad wouldn't let Mom out of his sight. He wanted her with him when he went on the road, and she did as he asked. I didn't resent my mother's absences as I had when I lived at Aloha Drive. Sure, I liked it better when she and Dad were around the house, but I didn't fall apart when they left. Why would I? Our house was infused with love and I felt secure even when they were gone. And when they were home, it was pure heaven.

During their long marriage, Mom and Dad became very close with two couples who'd known my mother for years, Dorothy and Bud Barish and Eleanor and Ray Moscatel. Mom and Eleanor had gone to college together and they'd been bridesmaids for each other. Ray started out as a professional basketball player. When Dad met him, Ray had left sports and owned a couple of bars in Seattle. Neither of the Moscatels watched "Bonanza," so Dad was an unknown to them. "Mike Landon" was simply Lynn's beau.

Mom brought Dad to Seattle to meet the Moscatels.

"They weren't married at the time," Ray told me, "and Eleanor and I were pretty prim and proper. Mike slept in the rec room in the basement while your mother stayed in the guest room. Mike was so young-looking. He was twenty-five and a few years younger than Lynn. He looked even younger, like a kid, really. And he was as eager to please as a kid, too. I remember we talked in the evening about mowing the lawn. I'd let it go for too long and was dreading the job. Well, the next morning I woke up to the sound of the mower. I looked out the window and there was Mike, mowing the lawn. He was a good kid, a real good friend."

Ray and Dad really got into mischief together. Dad thought Ray looked like Sean Connery and always played off the resemblance. When they were together and people would rush to get Dad's autograph, he'd sign and then say, "Gee, I'm only Michael Landon, but that guy's Double-Oh-Seven." They'd look over at Ray, see the likeness and go rushing to get his signature. Ray obliged and laughingly confessed, "I signed Connery's name, only I didn't know how to spell it. I'd wind up writing S-h-a-w-n Connery. Nobody seemed to notice the difference."

The Moscatels, Barishes, and Landons had some high old times together. They went out to dinner together at least once a week, sometimes all three couples and sometimes just two. Bud Barish told me they first met when Dad was playing Little Joe. Bud could see Dad was kind of a spunky guy with a short fuse. He said Dad was ready to fight with anyone if something struck him as wrong. A couple of times, Dad actually did get into fights with parking lot attendants.

Dad calmed down a lot due to Mom's influence. His temper didn't trip as easily. Some things, though, always bothered him and he'd react strongly. However belligerently Dad may have acted, he was a gentleman at heart and nothing infuriated him more than foul language. I'm not saying he didn't use strong words on occasion. He did, but he knew when to use them. Certainly he never wrote any scripts or routines that called for foul or dirty language.

One night my folks went with the Barishes to a restaurant in Beverly Hills. The people in the booth behind them were very raucous and through the din you could hear a lot of vulgar words being used, mostly by the men. The rude, loud talk continued, and Dad finally called over the waiter.

"Look," said Dad, "would you ask the people in the next booth to please watch their language because we're here with our wives."

The waiter did as Dad asked. The minute he'd finished talking, one of the men peered over the top of the booth and said, "What's the matter with you? Don't you like good English?"

Dad's face got beet-red. He looked at the guy and said, "If you use any more words like that, buster, you're going to be wearing them."

The guy stood up and so did Dad. Dad moved to get out of the booth and Dorothy Barish pushed her husband and said, "Get up there with him, Bud."

Dad stepped away from the table and the other man was making his way toward him when one of the women called out, "Hey, that's Michael Landon."

"I don't care who he is," shouted the guy.

"Oh, sit down and keep quiet. You don't want to get into a fight with Little Joe," said the woman.

The others with him urged the man to return to his chair. Dad was standing there ready and willing to slug it out, but he wasn't going to throw the first punch.

Reason prevailed and the man took his place. He and his friends even curtailed their loud comments.

Dorothy told me Dad became less likely to fly off the handle as the years went on because Mom was so even-tempered and considerate of others. He took his example from her. When Dad was interviewed by Barbara Walters in May of 1978, he said, "Everything I am today I owe to Lynn." (Barbara Walters considered her interview with Dad as one of her most disappointing. "He couldn't have been nicer," she said. "He was happy, easygoing, pleasant, but we never got through." She thought he "was afraid to reveal himself." Six months after that interview, Dad left Mom.)

The Barishes and Moscatels saw firsthand how much Mom meant to Dad. The six of them often spent weekends in Las Vegas, where Dad continued his practice of pretending his friends were some celebrity or other.

One night in Caesars Palace, he was called up to the stage and went to take a bow. Dad smiled and said he was so happy to be there with his friends, "Sean Connery and Nancy Sinatra." He waved over to the table and Ray got up along with Eleanor, who, indeed, did resemble Nancy Sinatra. Everybody applauded and later came over to get their autographs. "Shawn" and "Nancy" obliged.

Ray and Dad were incorrigible, and Dad definitely was the ringleader. Ray moaned that Dad egged him on.

"Your dad would think up the craziest schemes and drag me into it. One night, we all were at a party and one of the guests was a big Hollywood actor. We're sitting around having a good time when your dad comes over to me, throws a glance over to the actor and says, 'You know of course that guy is a Jew-hater.'

"I look up and say, 'What?'

" 'You heard me,' says Mike, 'the guy's a Jew-hater. I'm telling you he's a Nazi.'

"Okay, I take your dad's word for it and I go over and start getting testy with this guy. Like I'm baiting him, daring him to say something anti-Semitic so I can punch him one. Meanwhile, I look over at your dad and he's standing there laughing his head off. I walk over and say, 'Why the hell don't you get in this? You're Jewish. Stick up for me.'

" 'Listen,' says your dad, 'I was just kidding.'

"He was just kidding, and I'm practically starting a fistfight with this guy, who doesn't have a clue why I'm after him."

Dad frequently got Ray in hot water, especially with his wife, Eleanor.

"Poor Elly," said Ray, "after those zany episodes, she'd moan, 'You're ruining my life.' Gee, Mike loved to hear her say that. It was his favorite expression.

"See," Ray continued, "your Dad would set me up and I'd get in trouble. Even if I tried to do the same with him, somehow he'd wriggle out of it and I'd still be the patsy.

"One night we were in Vegas and it was hot, hot, hot. I'd just gotten a toupee and it was the first time I'd worn it. We were sitting at our table and Mike was staring at me.

" 'Whatta you lookin' at?' I said.

" 'Oh,' he said, 'I was just thinking how good that toupee looks on you.' Well, I'm real flattered and I felt great. Then we get up to go to the men's room. I walk in the door and the first thing I see in the mirror is Mike Landon standing next to a gorilla with hair growing from his eyebrows. The gorilla was me! Sweat had collected on my head and the toupee had been inching down my forehead all evening.

" 'Jeez, Mike, why the hell didn't you tell me?' I scream.

"And there's Mike doubled over, laughing and saying, 'But you looked *good*, Ray, you looked so *good*.' "

Ray, like all Dad's friends, thought Dad had everything. "Every facet of his life was full," Ray said on a more serious note, "he had the complete circle—the fun, the seriousness. He was brilliant, really brilliant, and kind, too. But if you ever crossed him, he would put you down very badly. He was witty and sharp-tongued. He never got me because when I saw he was in a bad mood, I'd go off. And he never played the star with me, either. He was just a pal."

Ray admitted he saw the changes taking place in my parents' marriage, yet he didn't think it would end the way it did. He remembered their last vacation trip to Hawaii together. Dad got really boisterous, which was so unlike him. He began making cracks and acting "ridiculous," according to Ray.

"He started getting loud," said Ray, "and Eleanor and Lynn were upset by his behavior. I said, 'You're acting dumb, Mike, you're embarrassing us. Go up to your room.' Well, he got up and went up to his room. Lynn went up after him and called to tell us he'd calmed down. The next day, he was his old self. But I sure was surprised to see him act so rowdy. It just wasn't like Mike. The man we knew bent over backward to make people feel good.

"I remember when Elly and I moved to Los Angeles into this duplex. I bought a stove and it was delivered to the front of the house. I had to get it up the walk and into the kitchen. Well, Mike came over and the next thing, he's got his shirt off and the two of us are lugging the stove into the house. Meanwhile, the neighbors catch sight of him and they're standing around watching with their eyes popping out. Here's Michael Landon moving appliances.

"Mike was really just a regular guy who happened to be a famous star. One of the best memories I have of your dad and mom is this: We'd just bought our home and it was still in escrow. Your dad and mom and Elly and I snuck into the house with pizzas and beer and we sat around on the floor laughing and talking. I think it was one of the happiest moments in my life and I know damn well a lot of that gladness came because your dad and mom were there."

Bud and Dorothy Barish also shared in the good times with Dad and Mom. Like the Moscatels, Bud and Dorothy weren't big television watchers and didn't know who Dad was at first. Dorothy and

Mom originally had met each other at a bridge game. Then, at a Christmas party, Mom went over to Dorothy and said, "You look terrific. When are you expecting?"

"I *had* the baby," Dorothy answered, and that was the beginning of their friendship.

"I thought I looked good after those pregnancies," Dorothy told me, "but Lynn could lose weight so fast after she delivered and I couldn't."

The Barishes and my folks became instant friends. The Barishes' children, Robert, Jr., and Laurie, were very close in age to Michael, Jr., and Leslie. We all lived in the same area and the children drew the families together even more.

The sextet of Landons, Barishes, and Moscatels enjoyed a lot of leisure time together. As Dorothy recalled, "Your dad was friendly and outgoing, more so than your mom. She was shy at that time and he did most of the talking. He told jokes like nobody else. Of course, your dad had more than one side to his personality and we were lucky enough to see the fun part."

Like the Moscatels, the Barishes were most impressed with Dad's firm sense of loyalty and friendship. Whenever they traveled together, all of them were treated as equals even though Dad was the star. Bud remembers a visit to Las Vegas that turned out a little different from most of their jaunts. Dad had been asked to appear at a cocktail party in Las Vegas. He asked the Barishes to join him and Mom.

"You've got to come," he said to Bud, "the whole thing's being comped. We got a suite with two bedrooms and all our meals and drinks and it won't cost a dime. You guys don't have to do a thing and all I have to do is go down to this cocktail party and mingle with the guests."

Bud and Dorothy thought it sounded great and the four of them flew off on the free weekend.

"Well," Bud reminisced, "the four of us went crazy. Mike would get up and say, 'Gee, I don't know whether to have salami and eggs or pancakes for breakfast. I guess I'll take both.' We wound up having eight breakfasts for the four of us and we had food and drinks coming every minute of the day . . . and night. We went to all the shows and danced and played tennis and had the best time.

"I think we were there for about four days and the only catch was that Mike had to appear at this promotional party on the last day.

The hotel people wanted celebrities around and were willing to pay for it. And that's all he had to do—no show, no anything, just attend the party and walk around and greet people.

"On the last day, someone called the room and said it was time for Mike to come to the party. Well, he said into the phone, 'I don't want to. I'm tired. I just don't feel like shaking hands with a lot of strangers. So the hell with it.'

"Mike didn't go to the party. Instead we went downstairs to check out and were presented with the entire bill for the stay. And what a bill it was, too! I mean, we'd been living like kings and queens. Mike looked at it, handed it to me and said, 'Well, I guess you and I will split this, Bud.'

"I was a bit shocked at first. I looked at Mike and saw he was serious. I didn't say a word and split the bill. Ordinarily I'd have been upset, but I couldn't be with Mike. Let me tell you, he was way ahead of everyone else when it came to picking up the check. You'd try to share, but he wouldn't let you. My luck, now he was going to let me. We split the check and that was that. Funny, all he had to do was walk around a room and shake hands, and for his own reasons, he just didn't want to do it."

Bud Barish also remembers how adoring Dad was of Mom.

"We'd sit down in a restaurant and Mike would say, 'I'll order this for my wife.' The rest of us didn't do that. Our wives ordered what they wanted and we ordered what we wanted. Then, at the table, they'd sit and hold hands and he'd start kissing her. It was something. We'd come home and Dorothy would say, 'I don't know why you can't be more like Mike.' When Mike pulled out, I remember turning to Dorothy and saying, '*See!*'

"With all that, I think of the nineteen years we knew Mike and Lynn, seventeen were perfect. And we saw them at least twice a week.

"Mike was great with the kids. That's where he really shone. Our son Robert was crazy about him. I remember when Robert was seven years old and kind of a little guy. Mike used to play ball with him and one afternoon he and Robert were playing football. Mike tripped and wound up spraining his ankle.

"That evening he went on the 'Tonight' show and Johnny Carson asked him what happened to his leg.

" 'Oh, I got tackled by Big Bob Barish,' answered Mike with a straight face.

"Let me tell you, our little Bob got such a kick out of being singled out as a 'big' guy, and on the 'Tonight' show, no less."

Robert Barish went to Tony Trabert's Tennis Camp with Leslie and Michael, Jr. Dad and Bud Barish would drive them up, and at the end of the session, go up and bring them home. Bud talked about their rides together.

"Mike's personality was so interesting. He had moods. Sometimes he'd talk so much you couldn't get a word in edgewise. Then there'd be times when he didn't say anything. So I'd try to start up a conversation and ask some questions. He'd give short answers and I knew he didn't want to converse. It wasn't hostile, he knew me and was comfortable with me. When he didn't want to talk, he just didn't. I accepted that. Gosh, I remember one trip up when I don't think he said two words.

"I'll tell you something, though, I think Michael had a hard time expressing himself as to how he really felt about things and people. But he had the ability to write what he couldn't say. He could do the most touching, wonderful, warm script.

"You knew when he was acting. When he was doing some kind of fund-raising, he'd go on television and he'd cry or do anything. But that was acting. When he talked to you on a personal basis, he didn't do that sort of thing. He wasn't emotional or anything like that. He didn't express his innermost feelings and I knew him for nineteen years. I knew him really well. And in all those years, I don't think we ever had an intimate conversation about anything. All that intimacy went into his writing."

Bud Barish was right about my dad's writing; his emotions streamed into his scripts. He was left-handed and wrote at such a fast pace, the result was legible only to his secretary. He'd start on a story and go right through to the end, sometimes staying up all night. If the script was heartrending, there'd be blotches of water sprinkled on the pages. Dad's work was so close to his heart, tears came to his eyes and spilled over onto the written page.

However reticent Dad might have been about sharing his innermost thoughts with intimates like Bud Barish, Dad's loyalty to his friends was unwavering. One time Dad was scheduled to be "roasted" on "The Dean Martin Show." "Roasts" were popular entertainment then, dinners at which a big celebrity would be feted, only instead of praising him to the skies, the assembled guests would go for the jugular—all in fun, of course.

Dad invited the Barishes to fly with him and Mom to Las Vegas and attend the show. The Barishes wanted to go, but there was no plane back that evening that could return them to Los Angeles and they had to be back in the city the next day.

"What are you talking about," said Dad, "you'll ride in the plane with us. Dean Martin has his own plane, a big 727, and we're going down with him."

The Barishes were a bit shy about doing this and Dad insisted.

"Listen, the only catch is, Dean usually doesn't like to have anyone go with him except those who are going to be on the show. So let me call him."

Dad telephoned and spoke to Dean Martin's representative.

"I'm bringing my friends with my wife and me," he explained. When the man at the other end said that no one except guests were allowed on the flight, Dad answered simply, "That's the only way I'll do the show."

Well, Martin's representative said he'd call back. He did and this time he made no bones about it.

"There's no way you're going to bring any other people. It's the rule. Dean doesn't ever want anybody on the plane except for a guest and maybe his wife, and that's it."

"Well," said Dad, "that's just too bad. I won't come."

"You can't do that, you've got a contract. We'll sue you."

"Look," Dad repeated, "you can do anything you want, but if my friends aren't on that plane, I'm not doing the show. You can cancel it."

Dad was strong, stubborn, and he wasn't afraid of anybody. Of course, they relented and Dad's friends were allowed on the plane.

Bud said it was like a fairy tale. They sat up front in this huge 727, which was empty except somewhere down in the tail section, where Dean Martin and his assistant were. They never even saw him on the flight.

On the way to Vegas, the stewardess brought them food and drinks, and while the others enjoyed themselves, Dad excused himself, saying, "I have to go over the script for the show tonight. I've got to get an idea of the cues." Bud watched as Dad began flipping through the pages. After a minute or so, Dad slapped the script down and said, "I can't do this."

"What do you mean?" asked Bud.

"I don't know who wrote this," answered Dad, pointing to the script, "but it's terrible. It's not me. I don't talk that way and I don't do this kind of thing. There's just no way I'm going to use this script."

"Mike," said Bud, "I don't know anything about show business, but don't you have to do it? I mean, when you feed the line to someone, don't they feed you back off the line? If you don't use the script, what's everybody else going to do?"

"It's their problem," answered Dad. "I'm a professional and I'll handle it."

Bud said he was really nervous while Dad was quite calm. Dad was dead set against the script and planned to wing it. Because the show was being taped in front of an audience, Bud didn't know what would happen and was scared to death that Dad would flounder, or, worse, make a fool of himself.

That evening Dad got up, did his own thing and was terrific. Not only did he handle himself beautifully, he rescued a number of other participants who were stumbling over their assigned lines. Bud said it went so much better than the original script would have. He had gotten a look at the script and understood why Dad wouldn't use it. First, it was terribly written, and second, some of the lines had Dad putting down Lorne Greene and Dan Blocker. Dad was being roasted that night and could take anything dished out, but no way would he talk down his friends.

Dad's energy was legendary. No matter where he went with Mom and their friends, he remained the "doer." He just couldn't sit still. Even on vacations, he was the first to rise and would make breakfast for the others. He had to be doing something, whether it was playing games or writing scripts. His friends remember walking into the room and seeing Dad sprawled on the floor using the coffee table as a desk and pouring words onto yellow legal-size pads of paper.

He began writing when the quality of the scripts for "Bonanza" took a nosedive. The plots were dull and the characters underdeveloped. Formula had taken over. Pernell Roberts rightly had complained about the substandard stories, but Dad didn't just complain, he tried to change things—and he did. Actually, in the mid-sixties, all the principals of "Bonanza" expressed disappointment in the scripts. Dad took advantage of the situation because he was very interested in the production end.

When scripts came in, he made suggestions and did some rewriting on the spot. His ideas were good and the producers latched on to them and eventually allowed him to create scripts himself. Within a short time, Dad was writing at least half the shows.

In 1968 he wrote one called *To Die in Darkness* and was given the opportunity to direct as well. Now he was an actor, writer, and director.

He loved directing and rated himself first a director, second a writer, and last, an actor.

These were the halcyon years of my parents' marriage. They fortified each other and enjoyed the company of their close friends. They even joined a country club, which was something Dad never thought he'd do. Dorothy and Bud Barish belonged to the El Caballero Country Club. One evening they brought Mom and Dad to a dinner dance. My parents had such a great time, they decided to join, which proved to be one of the best things that ever happened to me. There were dances, brunches, barbecues, pool parties, tennis tournaments, and golf games, and we took advantage of all of them and really enjoyed our membership.

I remember going to dinner dances and how much fun it was for me to get out on the dance floor. Dad didn't like to dance, he didn't think he was good enough. Still, he'd ask me to dance just to get *me* out on the floor. He was real proud of my dancing. Sometimes when I was on the rodeo tours with Mom and him, he'd be up on the stage and all of a sudden I'd hear him say something like, "And, my daughter Cheryl's a wonderful dancer. Would you like to see her?" There'd be a big round of applause and Dad would come and haul me onstage. And I'd dance in front of everyone. I wasn't embarrassed in the least because Dad was there. He made me feel that I could do anything. If Fred Astaire himself had ever dropped into El Caballero and asked me to dance, I'd have joined him in a flash. With Dad looking on, anything was possible. Actually, the chances of Fred Astaire showing up at El Cab were pretty slim.

My husband Jim reminded me of a funny story about Dad and El Caballero. Country clubs in Los Angeles were like country clubs everywhere, only more so. Some of them were pretty snooty, and a lot were restricted. Everyone knows the Groucho Marx classic about not wanting to join a certain country club because he didn't want to belong to any club that would accept him as a member. Well, though it didn't make any difference to Dad and Mom, El Cab happened to be a Jewish country club.

Dad entered a mini golf club tournament and was playing a round at one of the restricted clubs. Among the hosts were a couple of Catholic priests. Dad was in rare form and holding forth with jokes and stories and the priests were really taken with him.

"Now, Mike, you're a grand fellow," said one of them, "you're going to have to come and join this club. We can't let you go."

"Well, thanks, Father, that's really nice of you, but I already belong to a club."

"Oh, Mike, you're going to have to leave it and come to our club." The other priest joined in and started pressuring Dad, and so did the various members of the club who were present. They were pushing him to leave his club and join theirs.

"Jeez," Dad said finally, "it's so nice of you to ask me and I'd love to join you guys, but I told you, I already belong to a club."

"And what club might that be?" asked the priest.

"El Caballero," answered Dad.

"You're right, Mike, that's a good club. You better stay there," said the priest without blinking an eye. How Dad loved to tell that story!

After my parents' divorce, when I was so unhappy, I began to wonder if my parents had been as close as I thought. I questioned the Moscatels and the Barishes and they corroborated everything I thought I'd seen. They had witnessed my parents' total infatuation with each other. Ray remembered from the earliest days in Seattle how they'd be sitting in a restaurant talking and all of a sudden Dad and Mom would be gazing into each other's eyes, exchanging kisses, oblivious to everything around them.

"I'd make a joke about it," Ray confided. "I'd say, 'Mike, I'm talking to you, would you mind listening.' But they'd go on mooning over each other. It was really crazy; actually, it was kind of nauseating. And boy, did Elly and Dorothy get after me and Bud. 'Why can't you be like Mike?' they'd say to us. 'Look how he is with Lynn. Why, he doesn't even let her out of his sight for a minute.'

"And it was true. I mean, even if Lynn was just going to the ladies' room, Mike would follow her with his eyes all the way to the door. And, God forbid, any guy so much as took a look at her! He'd get furious. I never in my life have seen anyone so totally connected as those two."

With hindsight, you can see perhaps a slightly spooky aspect to Dad's behavior. He was so intensely bound to Mom, his judgment sometimes was affected, and he behaved outlandishly.

When Mom was pregnant with Mike, Jr., she started taking a knitting class at the Lanai Road School and went there a couple of times a week. Dad got suspicious of her being out, and decided she was having a rendezvous with a lover. So one day he actually drove down to the school to see if she was there. That day she happened to park her car in the back lot. When Dad didn't see Mom's car, he became convinced Mom was seeing someone else. He was ready to get a gun and shoot the "guy," when Mom and her companion came out of the school. Mom couldn't believe how he carried on.

"I was seven or eight months pregnant, for heaven's sake. What man would want to have an affair with me?" Mom laughed.

Actually, it wasn't funny. Dad was so crazy about her, she had to alter her behavior to keep him from going off the deep end. For instance, she rarely talked to other men when they were at parties. She didn't look at another man, and all because she knew Dad would start imagining all kinds of things and get hot under the collar. She just couldn't bear to hurt him, so she avoided any situation that might prove inflammatory. One thing's for sure, when they were together, they were *together*. Dad wouldn't leave her side.

Ray noticed that Dad changed after the divorce. "His relationship with his new wife was different," Ray told me. "I mean, we'd be at a party and Mike would come over and talk for a long time with me. Then he'd move off and talk to someone else. He barely looked to see what his wife was up to. I'm not saying he didn't love her, I'm just saying it was a whole other ball game."

Sometimes when Dad's friends talk about my parents' marriage, I think about how we children were "set up." When you see two people acting like Romeo and Juliet and it seems nothing on God's earth could ever get in the way of their love, and then it suddenly evaporates, well, it's very frightening. I know it was for me. It scared me about making a commitment myself.

8

When I entered Birmingham High School, I once more found
myself singled out as Cheryl "Michael-Landon's-daughter." By
now, I accepted the fact that some people would think I was "special" because my dad was a somebody; others might feel I was given
preferential treatment, and still others would assume *I* thought I
was hot stuff myself.

In a way, there's a little bit of truth in all of those assumptions.
You can't stick your head in the ground and pretend that nothing's
going on when your parent is on everybody's television screen.
Dad, however, set the example for all of us as far as interacting with
others. He didn't draw any distinctions among people except for
character. If you were a good person, a bright person, a fun person
with something to contribute, it didn't matter if you were a beggar
or a king. Many times, Dad would go to a fancy party or benefit and
wind up in the kitchen talking to the waiters.

I tried to follow Dad's lead and didn't rely on his renown to get
what I wanted. I didn't announce that Michael Landon was my
stepfather. I wanted to succeed on my own merits. And, give or
take a few mistakes, I think I did. Naturally, there were those who
took a different view. Most things went okay, although occasionally
there'd be a sticky situation.

I was involved in all sorts of school activities, and made pretty good grades, too. I was a language major and did really well in Spanish. I wasn't as good at algebra; in fact, I repeated that course in order to raise my grade. College was my goal and my marks had to be good. I was a senator in the student body's house of representatives and a leader in the girls' league program. I also worked as a teaching assistant with disabled children and found it inspirational.

It's essential for those of us who've been given so much to help those who are in need. That was one of my dad's firmest beliefs. We children were raised with the understanding that we were privileged and, in some way, had to share the wealth. We learned by watching Dad.

From the beginning, he never was too busy to go and help the less fortunate. He did some pretty wonderful things from his earliest days touring the rodeos, continuing right up to the era of "Us." Because of his high visibility, Dad could make a difference just by appearing for a charity, and he did, often. For every "good deed" that was publicized to benefit an organization, however, there were scores of activities that were never heard of. Dad wasn't looking for publicity; he was looking to help his fellow man. He was especially tuned in to children.

Dad's agent, Mike North, told me about a particularly moving incident that happened during "Bonanza's" heyday. Dad was at the Dixie National Livestock Show and Rodeo in Jackson, Mississippi. Mike North got a call from the Mississippi State Hospital, which was run by the University of Mississippi. They asked if Dad could come and visit the children's ward while he was in town. Dad said sure and they drove over to the hospital. One of the residents told Dad about a very special high school boy who was terminally ill with leukemia. After they got to the ward and visited for a while, Dad asked to see this boy, only to learn that he'd been sent home just before Dad arrived.

Dad and Mike went back to their hotel.

"All of a sudden," Mike told me, "your dad says, 'Call the hospital and find out that kid's name. Say we want to come and see him but we don't want any publicity—no papers, no TV, no press. We just want to go visit with him and his mom and dad.'

"So I called, got the name and telephoned the mother. Well, it turned out they lived about ninety miles south, in Columbia, Mississippi. When I told Mike where they were, he said, 'Okay, let's go.'

"The next day we drove to Columbia, and they'd followed instructions—there was nobody around, just this kid and his mom and dad. The boy was about six feet tall and I don't think he weighed one hundred forty pounds. We stayed all afternoon and your dad chatted and told stories and took pictures with the family. That kid never stopped smiling.

"We said our good-byes and after big hugs all around, we got into the car. Driving back, your dad was real quiet. All of a sudden I heard him sobbing. I turned around and said, 'What's wrong?'

"Your dad looked at me with tears streaming down his face and said, 'Why, Mike? Why does it have to happen to somebody like that?' "

Dad couldn't answer the question of why bad things had to happen to good people. He could only do his best to try to ease the suffering of those good people and to bring their plight to the attention of others. He did that *all* the time in *all* his shows.

So many episodes of "Little House" and "Highway" have to do with children suffering either physical or psychological pain, and those stories came out of Dad's exposure to the afflicted. In some cases, he even used the physically handicapped themselves rather than actors, and he was adamant about telling their stories honestly.

During the "Highway" years, Dad was often visited on the set by ailing children. He would talk to them as the "angel Jonathan" and answer their questions. The children were sent by various organizations, like the Make-a-Wish Foundation, the Starlight Foundation, and others that try to fulfill the wishes of terminally ill children. Dad was deeply affected by these meetings; they saddened him. At the same time he felt it was his duty to see the kids and answer their questions. He never refused them an audience. Most of the children wanted to know what it would be like when they died. Dad reassured them, and with his special combination of concern and humor, he'd make them feel better, at least while they were with him. "Jonathan" told them things would be okay, and they trusted him. How many children came to see him or how many he visited in hospitals over the years is impossible to reckon.

Dad was the personification of man's humanity to man and set the example his children were expected to follow.

★   ★   ★

While I enthusiastically worked with the disabled children, I also was a high school student and tried to have as much fun as possible. The high point of my extracurricular activities was my election as queen of the annual carnival in my senior year. I didn't campaign for the honor and was thrilled when it was announced. My joy, however, was dampened by some nasty rumors.

A couple of my classmates went around saying I was chosen because Michael Landon had given a big check to the school. I got wind of this and went to the principal. I told him I didn't want to be Carnival Queen. When he asked why, I explained that I wouldn't take anything that I hadn't earned for myself and if people thought my dad had bought me the honor, well, I wanted out.

The principal told me I was way off base. I'd been chosen because I was the most qualified. He absolutely refused to let me quit, and wisely said, "You have to believe in yourself, Cheryl. You were chosen because you won the competition."

I accepted the honor and enjoyed it.

During my high school years, Dad's popularity through his television shows grew and grew and grew. By the time I was graduated, he had become a household name. Newspapers and magazines were filled with stories about him and us. The Landons were cited as the "ideal family" and, to tell the truth, in many ways we were.

Not only were we a sturdy nuclear family unit, our strength extended to include Ginny Jean and Granddaddy John Noe. Dad loved both my maternal grandparents; indeed, he adored Ginny Jean. Without making a big deal about it, she was everything his own mother, Peggy, wasn't.

Once a reporter tried to get Dad to say something negative on the subject of mothers-in-law. Dad answered, "You don't believe those corny jokes, do you?"

The reporter replied that lots of mothers-in-law interfered, adding, "Most husbands have to deal with one."

"If they're lucky!" Dad said emphatically. "My mother-in-law is marvelous. She's a basic part of my family because she's a great human being. I could never forget what a blessing she is."

Needless to say, Ginny Jean was crazy about her son-in-law, having liked him from the beginning. At their first meeting, when Mom brought Dad over to her folks' house, Dad had been apprehensive. He said he felt "as if he were teetering on a tightrope over

Niagara Falls." He kept wondering if they would like him. He was afraid they'd think he was a "kook" because he was an actor. He wanted to seem as "normal" as possible and he wanted to please his prospective in-laws. He decided to bring Ginny Jean an appropriate gift. Aware of the Noes' Kentucky roots, he went to a music store and purchased an album called "Songs of the South" by the Norman Luboff Choir. He had the record gift-wrapped and clutched it in his hand as he and Mom drove to their destination. Dad kept asking, "Do you think your mother will like the album?" and Mom would reach out, pat his hand and keep reassuring him that she'd love it, and him too.

Dad was nervous as a cat, but all his fears were dispelled when he met Ginny Jean. She loved his gift and let him know it. He was completely charmed by her soft voice, her strong spirit, her sharp mind, and, of course, her irresistible Southern charm. He loved Granddaddy, too, and said of him, "I knew he wouldn't stand for any nonsense from me and I admired him for that."

The four of them went out for dinner and Dad amused and delighted my grandparents with his wonderful stories and his great humor. They got along beautifully. Dad later said he knew Ginny Jean was really at ease because she turned to him over dessert and asked, "Do you wear your hair that way for the show?"

Short hair was the fashion then, and obviously Ginny Jean had been eyeing Dad's long locks for the entire meal and building up her courage to ask him about it.

Dad laughed and explained that he'd been wearing his hair long since he was sixteen. Then he told about his "Samson complex." Ginny Jean listened attentively to the story of his javelin-throwing days, and at the end said she thought it was perfectly fine for him to wear his hair at whatever length he wanted.

Ginny Jean approved of almost everything Dad did, except for one thing. She thought he left the disciplining of us children too much to Mom. But she wasn't an interfering mother-in-law, and kept her own counsel. As Dad said in an article about his family:

My mother-in-law would never intrude, could never presume, because she has the swift sensitivity to the feelings of others I love in Lynn. They're wholly concerned when they can help. But they never pry into anything that's someone else's business, never hurt by gossiping. All their attention is on constructive encouragement. They don't think they have the right to live for another person, particularly the life of anyone dear to them. They look for the good they can see, express appreciation for it instead of stooping to phony flattery.

Dad praised Ginny Jean and Mom to the skies and talked about how lucky he and Granddaddy were:

John and I value their understanding, their intelligence. A man must have both in a wife—and a mother-in-law! The smart woman quickly notices a man's moods and adapts intuitively to them. Virginia will never drop in without phoning first to be certain it's absolutely convenient for us. Her politeness, her habit of never pushing aside the little courtesies, distinguishes her.

It sure did distinguish her, especially from Peggy O'Neill, who tried to ramrod her way into her son's life with those intrusive telephone calls.

Because Ginny Jean and Granddaddy never pushed, Dad and Mom eagerly sought their company. They took trips together and often went out in the evenings for dinner and the movies. Ginny Jean taught Dad how to play bridge and he liked it so much he had a green wooden pedestal card table with matching leather swivel chairs designed for our family room. Dad liked to win, and this was evident also at bridge. Commenting on his own acute need to prevail, Dad remarked, "Virginia and John and Lynn never get so wound up at cards they forget they're playing for the fun of it, so I try to recall this."

He may have tried to "recall" it, but it never changed Dad from being a fierce competitor in everything he undertook, from cards to sports, particularly tennis. When he and Mom played doubles, they *had* to win or Dad would get in a funk. He was very proud of Mom's athletic ability and she tried her darnedest because of him, even taking lessons. And although she got to be a very good player, she never had Dad's terrible need to win; she just liked to play. However, she knew how Dad felt, so she gave her all, more to make Dad happy than anything else.

Friends noticed Dad's extreme competitiveness, too. Bud Barish said, "When we played tennis, Mike so hated to lose, we actually wanted him to win. And he really put a lot of pressure on Lynn. She was good, but he wanted her to be the best."

Dorothy Barish added, "When we played doubles, it got to the point where I wanted them to win, and I'm competitive. But it meant so much to him, I wanted him to be happy." Dorothy thought what she said sounded a little silly, but Bud agreed, saying, "You felt bad if you beat him because he'd be down."

Dad loved golf. I remember one time when he was playing at a celebrity tournament and decided to impress the crowd. He pulled back for his swing so forcefully, the club hit the back of his head, nearly knocking him out.

The Barishes told me that Dad eventually dropped golf in favor of tennis. Though he wasn't a bad golfer, he got too down on himself if he didn't score low.

"Golf is a hard game," explained Bud, "because you play against yourself. In tennis you can miss a shot and still win. I think Mike gave up golf because the game beat him."

Most of the people who competed with Dad felt the same way—they didn't want him to lose because it made him so unhappy. Those who loved him accepted his behavior. Ginny Jean saw how much winning meant to Dad, too. When they played bridge, he'd do anything to get the controlling hand. The bottom line was, Dad could handle competition only one way—he had to win.

Among the many things Dad especially admired about my grandmother were her strong religious convictions. My grandmother is a staunch Presbyterian, and when Mom's and Dad's kids were born, Dad thought they should be baptized in her faith.

"I felt the children should have the opportunity for religious knowledge and I couldn't think of a better example of religion in action than Virginia," said Dad.

And so Dad had children being brought up in the Jewish faith (Dodie's kids), the Catholic faith (me), and as Protestants (Leslie, Michael, Shawna, and Christopher). We were about as ecumenical a family as you can get under one roof.

Dad used to tell the story about when he and Mom were first dating and he was still a bit shy with her folks and occasionally would get a little tongue-tied. They went for a ride with Granddaddy and Ginny Jean and were driving in the area of my other grandparents' home. Dad commented on the number of Catholic churches.

"Wow, Virginia," he said to Ginny Jean after they'd driven past the umpteenth Roman Catholic church, "I'll bet you're the only prostitute in this neighborhood."

I don't know who loved to tell that story more, Dad or my grandmother.

Dad's affection for his in-laws extended to their relatives. He and Mom went to Kentucky to visit Ginny Jean's mother, my great-grandmother, Virginia Plock. Nanny lived with a housemate, Mattie Clark. Both women were widows, and they had decided to sell their houses, combine their furnishings, and live together in a cozy house in Louisville, not far from Ginny Jean's sister, Lynwood Kern, our beloved Aunt "Woo." Aunt Woo often came and stayed with us kids when Dad and Mom were traveling. They were glad to put us in her care because we adored her and she felt the same about us. I'm so lucky. Ginny Jean and Aunt Woo are still going strong. They're not even shy about telling their ages. My grandmother is in her early eighties and Aunt Woo is ninety-one. Each is as sharp as a tack and as active as can be. Both of them drive cars and do their own shopping.

Dad got the biggest kick out of Nanny Plock. He loved the fact that she had picked up with Miss Mattie and the two had created a whole new living place. And he couldn't get over the way the two women adapted. Lifelong Methodists, they decided to be baptized anew in the Baptist church simply because it was located right across the street.

On his first trip to visit Nanny, Dad drove her downtown to keep him company while he shopped for a pair of shoes.

When the people in the store saw "Little Joe," they gathered around. Soon Nanny and he were surrounded by enthusiastic fans of "Bonanza." The attention, naturally, centered on Dad, but one fan turned to the elderly lady with him.

"Who are you?" he demanded of Nanny.

"I'm Ma Cartwright!" she exclaimed.

My great-grandmother was full of spirit throughout her life. In 1970, for her ninetieth birthday, Dad brought her out from Louisville to visit us in Los Angeles. He didn't want her to make the trip alone, so he paid for Miss Mattie to come out too. And he also brought out Aunt Woo and her husband, Arthur. As if that weren't enough, he put them all into "Bonanza"!

He wrote and directed an episode in which Hoss was going to shoot at somebody. He had Aunt Woo and Uncle Art standing in a doorway while Nanny and Miss Mattie sat in rocking chairs on the porch of the Ponderosa. None of them had any speaking lines, and the only acting required of them was to look scared when Hoss drew his gun.

Nanny and Miss Mattie were as excited about being on camera as any starlets. They were giggling away as the dressers got them into costumes. After they were decked out in frontier garb, the announcement came over the loudspeaker that Mr. Landon was ready for them. Suddenly Nanny and Miss Mattie both had to go to the bathroom. Aunt Woo took them, in costume, to the lavatory. It took them a little while because of the elaborate clothing they were wearing. When they finished, they returned to the set and did the scene. They had fun and what a great story to tell their friends.

Dad continued to visit Nanny whenever he was in or around Louisville. One time he was on his way to the races and he decided to drop by and visit. He came into Nanny's room and found her dozing in her rocker, so he pulled up a chair and sat down beside her. When she opened her eyes, he asked gently, "Is there anything I can do for you?"

"Yes," replied Nanny, "go have your hair cut."

Dad told her he was going to the races and asked her what number horse he should pick.

"Number seven!" said Nanny emphatically.

Dad went to the track, bet on number seven and won. He called Nanny and told her that half of what he got was hers.

Gosh, we had such wonderful, wonderful family times. I think, perhaps, the most special were the Thanksgiving and Christmas feasts at Ginny Jean's. My grandmother made the *best* turkey ever, and we will swear to that.

I have to say, even after Dad and Mom were divorced and Dad became less than gracious about my mother, he never lost his affection for Ginny Jean. And despite her deep dismay and sadness when Dad divorced Mom, my grandmother retained a soft spot for her ex-son-in-law. So did Aunt Woo, who, like all of us, was brokenhearted over the divorce.

"I was very disappointed in him," she told me recently, "but there were so many wonderful things that he did. He was a very generous and gracious man, and such a lot of fun. I will not say ugly things about him. I try to think of the good things."

Like Aunt Woo, all of us try to think of the good things.

9

In my teens, when I began dating, my parents kept a close watch over my social activities. They claimed they weren't overprotective, and maybe they weren't, but you'd have a hard time convincing most of the guys I dated. Naturally, there were ground rules; among the most important was the "return" hour. Dad and Mom were very strict about what time I got in. Even when I had a "steady" boyfriend who was known to them, I still had to be back before eleven o'clock. Even though I was the daughter of a television star, my dating pattern was about the same as any small-town girl's.

Before I was old enough to go on real dates, Dad used to drive me and my girlfriends to parties, and pick us up, too. Then we began double-dating, and still the chauffeur was Michael Landon. Even when I became old enough to go out on my own, he watched out for me. I honestly didn't mind. I never felt he was interfering; he had that wonderful way of showing interest and making you feel good about yourself. I could confide in him without worrying he'd laugh at me. I told him about all my crushes and he never made fun of me or put me down. He didn't try and compete with my boyfriends either, and he sure could have!

Dad was in his mid-thirties and in wonderful shape; he easily could have passed for an underclassman. He was, however, the father figure and assumed all the responsibilities that position called for. Dad never forgot his own experiences in dating. He remembered his own background and applied it to current situations. He wouldn't make anyone feel as miserable as he was made to feel by so many of the parents back in Collingswood. He always tried to put my dates at ease, and yet was very firm about what was expected of them.

One time, I was picked up to go dancing and my date was talking to my dad when I came into the room.

"Now run along and have a good time, you two," Dad said, adding, "and be sure and get Cheryl home by eleven o'clock."

"Are you kidding?" asked my date. "You're not serious about that time business, are you? It's a joke, right?"

"A joke?" said my dad. "I don't joke about things like that, young man. I said be back by eleven o'clock and I mean it. And by the way, in case you get absentminded, you'll see me waiting in the driveway for you." We got home on time but you can be sure he would have been waiting in the driveway had we been late.

A lot of the boys I dated complained that when they were introduced to Dad, he'd give them a knuckle-crunching handshake.

"My dates say you use an awfully strong grip," I said.

"I know I do," smiled Dad, "I'm doing it on purpose. I just want to let them know who they're dealing with."

Despite the fact that we were given just about everything we wanted, within reason, of course, Dad and Mom firmly believed we kids should earn our own money. I had taken typing in junior high school and, later, was employed in my father's law office. I still saw my father and his family, though not on a regular basis. I would visit on an occasional weekend and spend some holiday time with them. Even though I was a conscientious worker and barely took lunch breaks, working for my father proved to be no easier than living with him. I didn't last too long in the office.

One afternoon, I was scheduled to go to my grandfather Angelo's birthday party. Dad Landon wanted to see me regarding some personal thing that needed immediate attention. I called my father and told him I was going to be a little late to my grandfather's celebration. I told him I was going to see Michael Landon and my father shouted, "Don't bother coming to the party and don't bother coming to the office. You're fired!"

How Dad loved his little "Les," "Lester," or "Louie," all nicknames he used for Leslie. Here they are on vacation in Acapulco, Mexico.

Dad took this picture of me, off the coast in Mexico. Fishing was the first sport Dad taught me.

Dad would do almost anything to get Leslie to eat her dinner, and it usually worked! You can see why.

Here Leslie and I are standing in front of the famous lava waterfall in the yard of our Encino house. This is the wall Dad climbed up barefoot, wielding his flyswatter against the bees who had invaded from next door.

We spent some of our summers at Laguna Beach, south of Los Angeles. We had the ground floor of the building you see behind Dad and Leslie. To little girls like Leslie and me, those summers were awesome!

Dad and Nany, my great-grandmother. She was a great lady and a true Southern belle. She and Dad adored each other. One day when she was out with Dad, a fan came up and asked Nany, "Who are you?" "Why, I'm Ma Cartwright!" she replied.

Another Acapulco vacation shot, with me in my intense baby-fat period. Dad, however, obviously no longer needed his "Ugey" body pads; he was well built and strong by now.

Some of my happiest memories are from the time we had together in the Encino home. Here I am at Christmas time with Mom, Dad, Mike Jr. held by our nanny, Olive, and Leslie.

This photo is a souvenir of our trip to Texas to visit NASA headquarters, where I got to meet many of the astronauts.

Dad with my brothers Josh and Mike Jr., and Leslie and me in the backyard of our Encino "Camelot."

One of the great things about being a part of a celebrity family was getting invited to ride in the Christmas parade. Dad loved his fans, except when they got so excited they tried to tear off his clothes. Fortunately that didn't happen very often.

How Dad loved his girls! And how we loved him! In addition to Leslie and me, there was a more recent arrival—Shawna.

No, this is not the result of Mom's cooking. This is Dad on the "Bonanza" set, doing one of his stunts himself, something he liked to do whenever possible.

Two shots of Mom and Dad at Las Vegas. In the photo on the opposite
page they are with their best friends (left to right), Ray Moscatel, Bud and
Dorothy Barish, and Eleanor Moscatel. In the picture above they have
brought me along, as well as some of my closest friends—Jeff, Jessie, and
Robby. What a treat for a group of teenagers!

Dad on the set of the Mike Douglas Show. This was the talk show on which Mom was introduced and was so nervous she walked up to Dad, shook his hand, said "Nice to meet you," and walked off the set.

I never saw two people more in love than Mom and Dad. Dad once told Mom that no matter what, he would never love anyone as he loved her.

When we moved from Encino to Beverly Hills, a lot of things changed, not the least of which was the extravagantly furnished and appointed dining room. For a good while, however, the laughter remained the same.

Cheryl dear – We're so happy you're doing so well. Keep up the progress!

A.G. Gyles

Me too!!! Mrs. (Bill) Cagney

Jim Cagney

you get well soon – we love you –

Jonathan Winters

me Too!

Nancy Morgan

Me Too, Too – Al ne Bellamy

Cheryl dear –
I make house calls!
"Doc" Billy Stone

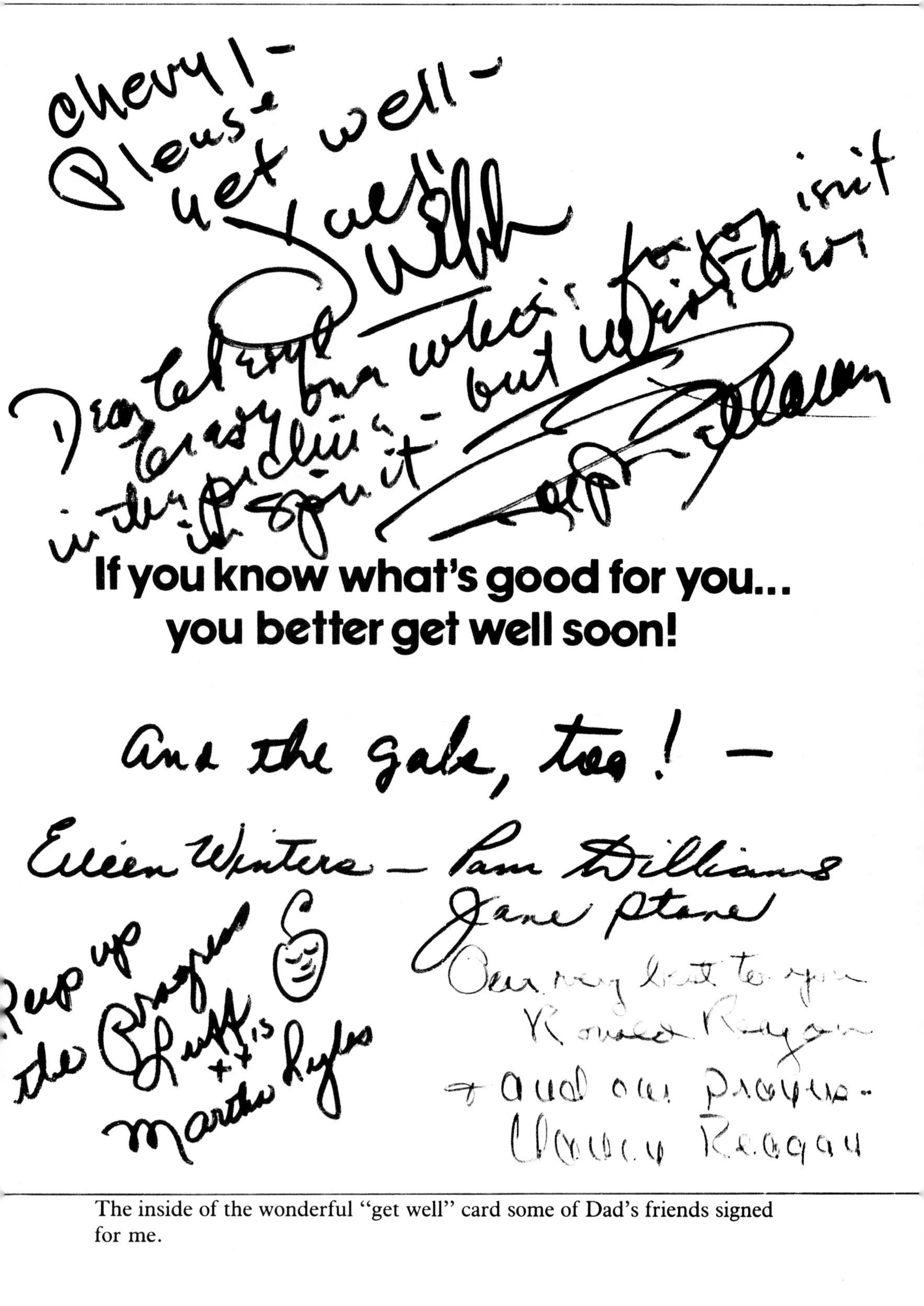

Cheryl! –
Please –
get well –

[handwritten signatures, largely illegible]

If you know what's good for you...
you better get well soon!

And the gate, too! –

Eileen Winters – Pam Williams
Jane Stone
Our very best to you
Ronald Reagan
+ and our prayers –
Nancy Reagan

Keep up
the Prayers
+ it is
Martha Rafer

The inside of the wonderful "get well" card some of Dad's friends signed for me.

Ginny Jean, General John, Mom and Dad on one of their many vacations together—this one in the Hawaiian Islands. Dad had the most unusual relationship with his in-laws; they loved being together and socialized frequently.

Mom tells me now that when this photo of "the perfect Hollywood couple" was taken, she was in great emotional pain, because at this point she was aware that Dad was having an affair with a woman who was a stand-in for the character Mary on "Little House on the Prairie." Sometimes pictures do lie.

★   ★   ★

In my senior year at Birmingham, I only had classes in the morning. Aside from homework, my afternoons were free. Dad was very busy with his acting, writing and directing. He didn't have a secretary to handle his fan mail, and I had all those secretarial skills to use, so I offered to help out by working part-time. Dad was delighted and set up a little office for me at Paramount where he did his filming. I did a lot of essential chores for my dad and like to think I made things easier for him.

It wasn't all work and no play, by any means. I had plenty of time to enjoy myself, too. Birthdays were extra-special occasions. I'll never forget my sweet-sixteen party at El Caballero. It was fabulous, and at the end Dad took me out the main door and handed me the keys to a brand-new Corvette parked in the driveway. He was so happy to be *giving* me such a splendid present, there were tears in his eyes. I was crying too, because I was *getting* the present.

Dad was extravagant. The night of my senior prom, he and Mom hired a plane and flew me and my boyfriend and another couple to Las Vegas to celebrate.

Yes, it's pretty heady stuff for a girl to have her own car at sixteen and at seventeen to be whisked off to Las Vegas for an evening. I guess I could do and get just about anything I wanted. Certainly that was part of the "spoiling."

Frankly, I can't say whether it's good or bad to indulge your family when you have the means to do so. I guess it's a combination of good and bad. I was treated like a princess, and when you get used to a certain way of life, it's hard to accept anything less.

I don't think my dad could refuse us any material thing; he wanted, perhaps even needed, to give us all the things he'd been denied. At the same time, he wanted us to be self-reliant. So we were urged to get out there and do things, to learn to be independent. Yet at the same time we were smothered with excesses. In one sense, by showering us with luxuries, Dad was making us into the kind of people he didn't want us to be.

How can you be independent when you're given everything you need and frequently more than what you need? What's the sense of struggling when you're really not striving for anything? More than anyone, I think my mother fell into that trap. She'd always been self-reliant and had worked right along with Dad, inspiring and

97

encouraging him. During my high school years, Dad was riding high, even though "Bonanza" was winding down. I read somewhere (he'd never have told me) that he was making around ten thousand dollars a week as Little Joe. By the time I was in college, "Bonanza" was gone and Dad was working on a new television series based on the *Little House on the Prairie* books by Laura Ingalls Wilder.

Ed Friendly, the television producer, bought the rights to the Laura Ingalls Wilder series, which had been entertaining readers for almost half a century. He developed a "Movie of the Week" pilot from the material and brought it to my dad. Dad brought it home to Mom and she became very involved with this project. She loved the books and was enthusiastic about his doing the show. They spent long hours going over ideas and details together. When Dad presented the show to NBC as splendid family entertainment and a perfect vehicle for him as the head of the Ingalls family, the network bought it, although they weren't sure it would make it.

On March 30, 1973, *Little House on the Prairie* was televised and received the highest rating in the NBC "Movie of the Week" category. Little wonder that NBC immediately decided to produce a "Little House" series.

Dad became executive producer, star, director and writer of this enormously popular show. One critic wrote that with "Little House," Dad "single-handedly was able to create and shape the visions in his own dreams and deliver them into the reality of a strong, successful weekly television family drama." Everybody loved "Little House." Dad knew instinctively that the time was ripe for a good old-fashioned program with clear-cut values, in which family and friendship were the abiding themes.

Dad meticulously assembled a superb cast and crew for the run of the program. They became a family. Dad literally became a surrogate father for Melissa Gilbert, who began playing Laura when she was nine. I think I have a pretty good idea of how she felt about Dad, since I was almost her age when I became his real daughter. Melissa spent a lot of time with our family and has remained close to my sister Leslie.

Melissa adored my dad and was as astounded as we Landons were when Dad left Mom. Recently she commented in *People* magazine that Dad was "a remarkable man who just wanted a solid, loving family, so he had three." She went on to say how much she looked up to him, but "any man who leaves his wife of eighteen years for someone who worked on his show is not a perfect person." You see, Dad's professional "children" were as distressed as his real children by his action.

A total of two hundred and four episodes of "Little House" were filmed, and every one of them bears the stamp of Michael Landon. They stem not only from the pen of Laura Ingalls Wilder, but from the dream of Ugey Orowitz for a family whose members wouldn't be afraid to show their love for each other and who would stand up collectively for what they believed was right.

"Little House" ran from 1974 to 1982. During that time, the Ingallses lived from hand-to-mouth, but the Landons began to live lavishly. In the mid-seventies, when great success came to Dad, he used his wealth to create a luxurious life-style for his family.

10

I entered the University of Arizona at Tucson. It was my first time away from home and the transition went well, although naturally there were initial problems. Dad and I had discussed my curriculum and he felt that since I wasn't math- or science-oriented, I should major in drama. I talked about being an actress, but it was mostly talk. I really loved to dance and was quite a good dancer, and I think if I had opted for any career at that moment, it would have been in dance. No matter what I might have wanted to do in terms of performing, at this point in my life I wasn't going anywhere except to college. Dad thought it was fine that I liked dancing and acting and didn't rule them out, but he was absolutely firm about my finishing school before I looked into any profession.

Following Dad's suggestion, I majored in drama, with a minor in speech. In the theater division, I fell into a trap. Members of the drama department assumed that Michael Landon's daughter was going to be a pro. In truth, my acting experience was limited to the spontaneous skits we performed on our family theater nights at home. I was expected to be a Sarah Bernhardt simply because my father was an actor. Well, I wasn't any Bernhardt. I was terrified when auditions were held and I had to get up in front of everybody and act. My knees were knocking and my heart was pumping. But somehow I got through it and managed to land a small part in a production of the Shakespeare play *The Taming of the Shrew.*

I remember acting opposite a guy who was out to prove he wasn't impressed by my father. During our scene together, this fellow had to kiss me. At the first rehearsal, he came at me like a drooling idiot and slobbered all over my neck. I heard him chuckling under his breath as he wiped his mouth over my skin. He was going to show Michael Landon's daughter a thing or two. I didn't want to push him away or make a big to-do, so I just gritted my teeth.

When the scene was finished, I wiped off my neck and started back to the sorority house, very upset by the way I'd been treated. I was naive about rehearsal schedules, too. I didn't know the scene had to be repeated, or that the instructor was looking for me.

The next day, when I walked onto the stage, the teacher came up to me. Instead of taking me aside and explaining how rehearsals were run, he screamed at me in front of everybody. I was humiliated. The gist of the tirade was: Who the hell did I think I was? Just because I was Michael Landon's daughter, did I think I could do what I pleased? He tore into me and my confidence was shattered. I most certainly hadn't flaunted my father's name.

Part of the hardship of being a celebrity's child is living up to the enormous expectations others project upon you. And if I didn't respond correctly, I was deemed spoiled rather than naive. I realized at this point that teaching would be more fulfilling and I added education to my major.

At first, I couldn't completely shake the Michael-Landon's-daughter syndrome. During rush week I was walking to a sorority house and someone called out, "Hey, that's Michael Landon's daughter." A bunch of them began singing "dum dede dum dede dum dum dum dede"—the "Bonanza theme"—then they went on to parody some Beach Boy lyrics to the effect that "she'll have some fun, fun, fun till her daddy takes her Corvette away." I didn't think it was funny or particularly nice. I was embarrassed and tried to ignore them.

Things got better once I joined Delta Gamma. I was fully accepted by my sorority sisters, and had such a great social life that it made up for almost all the conflicts in other areas.

One of my closest sorority sisters, Joyce, lived in Phoenix. During spring break of my freshman year, I went home with her to visit her family. We had a great time just hanging around. I thought it would be fun for us to go to a local woman who had extrasensory powers. Some of Joyce's friends had been to this psychic and she'd told them their futures—how many children they were going to have, and whom they were going to marry. I was very curious to know what my future husband might be like.

Joyce and I went to the psychic's house and were greeted by a perfectly ordinary-looking and quite pleasant woman. The only thing out of the ordinary was her attire; she had on a black robe with a white collar. Joyce went first. The psychic took her into another room while I sat down in the waiting area. A short time later, Joyce returned. She was smiling and seemed excited. It made me excited, too. I eagerly followed the psychic through the door. We went into a room scarcely larger than a closet and sat down in two chairs facing each other.

"Now, dear," the psychic said, "I'm going to go into a trance." All of a sudden she began shaking, really shaking.

"This is strange!" she said. "This rarely happens." Her voice started deepening. "Something's happening to me. Don't do anything. Don't touch me," she admonished. "If I fall on the ground, let me lie there. It's just going to happen. Let me be."

With these words, the shaking became more violent. Her eyes closed and she clenched her fists and brought them to her face. Her skin had turned bright-red and weird noises came from her lips. I was terrified. I didn't know what to do. It seemed as though we sat there forever.

Then, as suddenly as she had passed out, she came to. Her eyes popped open and she looked straight at me and began to speak. "My dear child, I have to tell you that something terrible is going to happen." Her tone was kindly but grave and my heart began to pound as she continued. "There is going to be a very bad car crash in the fifth month. I cannot say if you will be involved in the accident itself, but you will be affected by it."

I was very upset. I had come on a whim to find out whom I was going to marry and now I was hearing a horror story about an automobile accident. I couldn't wait to get out of there.

As I was leaving, the psychic looked me straight in the eye, touched my forehead with her hand, and said, "May God bless you. Call me after it happens."

I was really shaken up. I phoned my mother that evening and

told her what had happened. Mom said to forget about it, and so I did. I forgot all about it until May of 1973.

During my freshman year at college, my mother and dad decided to move.

Our Encino home, which had been exactly right for us, now seemed too small, too out-of-the-way, too "humble." We had lived there for over ten years and had blended into our surroundings, had become part of the community. Sure, some people still turned to look and stare at Michael Landon, and some wanted autographs, but anyone who approached him that way was an outsider, not a neighbor. We lived comfortably but not ostentatiously. Then, when Dad became a mega-star during "Little House," he began to think of "moving on up." He needed a showcase home, and, boy, did he buy one! We went from rambling ranch in Encino to majestic mansion in Beverly Hills. It was spectacular.

The estate had been designed by Paul Williams and was perched on a hill above Beverly Hills. The property was completely walled and had electric security gates. The grounds were terraced and manicured, with rolling lawns, many trees, and flower gardens that bloomed all year round. The house itself had a two-story formal entryway and a double-curved staircase. There were parquet floors, wainscoting, and an elaborate crystal chandelier. The entranceway had a huge stained-glass window Mother had had made especially. It was inscribed "I Love You More Than Yesterday But Less Than Tomorrow, Pumpkin." "Pumpkin" was Mom's pet name for Dad.

The step-down living room had raised wood-paneled walls, fancy moldings, a marble fireplace, and a Chippendale chandelier. The dining room had crown moldings, recessed lighting, and also a fireplace.

There were seven bedrooms in the main house, and adjoining housekeeper's quarters for two. Mom and Dad's master suite was in its own wing and had a fireplace, an adjoining study, dressing rooms, walk-in closets, and his and hers baths. Everything you could imagine was there, including an enormous heated swimming pool with two cabanas and an imposing poolside entertainment center which had a large custom-paneled room with high beamed ceilings, a fireplace, chandelier, wet bar, kitchen and bath. There were also a custom-built tennis court and air-conditioned brick tennis house complete with cooking facilities and bathroom.

On the "informal" side, there was a special recreation room which was created to give the feel of the Old West, called the "Bonanza" room, in tribute to the show that had been the start of the journey that brought us to this splendiferous castle. Wood-paneled, with a beamed ceiling and leaded glass windows overlooking the gardens, this room had an unusual fireplace made of copper.

Oh, and I don't want to forget the oval breakfast room and the professionally equipped kitchen. And besides the ten-car brick motorport, there was a three-car garage.

Believe me, the house was breathtaking.

A home doesn't break up a marriage, so I can't blame our new house for what happened later. Looking back, though, I remember having strong misgivings about the move.

Naturally, in Beverly Hills our life-style changed. You cannot live in such obvious splendor without being affected. No more those wonderful excursions to Barone's for pizza, holiday dinners at the Noes' house and our days at El Caballero. Now we had servants right and left, and, in some cases, those servants were stealing from my parents left and right! No kidding. One couple literally handed cases of Dad's liquor out of their bedroom window to accomplices waiting outside. I saw it with my own eyes. Our extravagant surroundings caused extravagant problems. Other servants cashed illegal checks and stole jewelry. One couple pawned Dad's watch and stole Mom's 10-carat diamond ring. When my parents found out, they brought charges against the couple.

Crooked servants aside, eventually everyone adjusted to the new surroundings with real enthusiasm. Ginny Jean, whose feet were firmly planted in the earth, thought the Beverly Hills house was the most glorious place in the world. She was so proud of Mom's and Dad's success; she'd bring her friends over and show them the house.

In many ways we were as happy in our new home as we had been in the old, but everything seemed to be done on a much "grander" scale. We still indulged in family sports matches, theatrical evenings, and pranks. Dad still loved to play with the little ones. He'd make up scenarios involving an alien from outer space named Spaun. Once Dad took Shawna and Chris with him to watch Spaun land in his spaceship on our property. The three of them crept down the staircase, out the door, and into an alcove in the driveway. Shawna and Chris eagerly awaited the arrival of Spaun.

"There he is! " cried Dad. At that moment he blasted an air horn he'd hidden behind his back. The two little ones jumped a mile!

Dad loved to play monster. One evening he was chasing Leslie and Michael around the master bedroom suite. He let out a huge roar and raced into the bathroom, where my brother and sister were hiding. The floor was wet and Dad slipped and slid through the plate-glass window. The splintered glass ripped his foot open and blood was everywhere. Mom and I rushed to the bedroom when we heard the crash.

"Lynn," Dad shouted, "get me some cloth, quick. I need a tourniquet." Mom ran into the bedroom and ripped the sheet off the bed. She tried to tear the sheet into workable pieces but was so hysterical she couldn't start a rip. I sat next to Dad and watched as he calmly tried to make his own tourniquet by using towels. The governess drove them to the hospital. Dad was calm and collected; Mom was in a panic. Everything turned out fine. The "monster's" foot was sewn up and quickly healed.

11

One of my favorite Delta Gamma sisters was a soft-spoken up-perclassman named Cathy Stubbins. Cathy had been my pledge mother when I entered the sorority and was a great friend and a big help in getting me settled in at college. She guided me when I needed to be shown the ropes, and always accomplished it in the nicest way possible. She was thoughtful and kind as well as fun to be with. If I was feeling down, she'd leave gifts for me. Not big things, maybe just a card or a stuffed animal, or a silly gadget . . . whatever. The important thing was, Cathy Stubbins was a warm, loving, and admirable person. I looked up to her. And Delta Gamma was a fun place to be; I loved college and especially the time spent with the sorority. I had an opportunity to hold a few offices, and I worked very hard at my studies. And of course, we sometimes partied hard too.

As the second semester of my sophomore year was drawing to a close I felt especially blessed. It had been an exceptionally wonder-ful year, one of the happiest I'd ever experienced. The awkward-ness of adjusting to being away from home, of being exposed to the celebrity-relative hostility of some of my classmates—all that was behind me. I really belonged at last. I was doing well in my studies, and I had a pretty active social life, dating nobody special, but meeting a lot of neat guys.

Sigma Alpha Epsilon, a popular fraternity, had scheduled a big celebration one evening in May and I was one of their little sisters. They planned a day-long salute to a gentleman named Paddy Murphy, supposedly a notorious Chicago mobster of the twenties who had once hidden out in the old SAE Chapter house in Tucson where he was supposedly "rubbed out."

The afternoon of the festivities, SAE members wore spats and pinstripe suits and rode in a long funeral procession behind a silver limousine carrying an empty coffin. The whole event was an inane fraternity prank, the kind of thing kids do to have a good time. To top off the day, a party was to be held in an old ranch house way out in the desert.

Cathy Stubbins was going with her steady boyfriend, Michael Van Woy, the head of the physical education department at Morningside High School in Inglewood, California. Cathy had met Michael's friend Dennis Albright, the assistant football coach at Morningside.

"I got a nice fellow for you," she told me a few weeks before the SAE party. "He works at Morningside with Mike and I think it would be great if the four of us went to the frat party together. What do you say?"

I said yes. Blind dates can be tricky, but I figured if Cathy thought this guy was okay, I'd probably like him. I trusted her judgment. I wrote "Date w/Stubbins and her Mike to S.A.E. party" on the calendar hanging over my desk.

The evening of the party, a bus had been hired to take everyone to the ranch house in the desert. There was sure to be a lot of drinking, and the sororities and the fraternities often arranged for transportation to cut down the possibility of drunk driving. I'd told my dad and mom about the party, of course, and they were reassured to hear that the driving would be left to professionals.

The bus came and all the partygoers got on—except for Cathy and me. Our dates hadn't arrived yet, so we had to send the bus off without us. Funny, you don't think about the piling up of coincidences when they're happening. It's only when you look back that you realize how fate works.

Not long after the bus left, Mike and Dennis drove up in a blue

Volkswagen. They were apologetic; they'd just been delayed by traffic. There was nothing we could do except get in the car and head into the desert.

Dennis seemed to be a nice guy. I looked forward to a pleasant evening.

The party was being held in an old ranch house that wasn't a part of the University. I remember it was a good long drive to get there, almost two hours. The place was jumping when we arrived and we joined right in. People were dancing and singing and there was a lot of beer drinking.

When the evening wound down and the time came to go home, most of the kids piled into the bus. Cathy, Dennis, Mike and I got into the Volkswagen. I have to be honest. We'd all been drinking and were definitely feeling the effects. I was pretty giddy, but then, I wasn't driving. Mike and Cathy wanted to get into the back seat, so Dennis took the wheel. He seemed to be okay, although I was in no condition to judge. I slid into the front seat next to him.

We drove off toward the highway. I remember that it was very dark; there were no streetlights or any kind of illumination to speak of, just the gleam of our own headlights to show us the way.

We reached the highway. Dennis drove onto the entrance ramp and looked down the road. Nothing was there. He put his foot on the gas and pulled out onto the road. The car lurched forward and, suddenly, stalled. Everything went dead, including the headlights.

Cathy and Mike couldn't have cared less. They were involved with each other in the back seat. Dennis turned the key and stepped on the gas pedal.

And then it happened.

While Dennis was trying to start the car, another vehicle came barreling down the highway, going eighty miles an hour. At the wheel was a drunken driver. It was so dark, and our lights were out, so he never saw us. I don't know if he'd have seen us had our lights been on; all I know is what I was told later.

The driver never touched his brakes; he crashed full-force into us. Our car went hurtling down the deserted road. We were propelled the length of a football field and flipped over and over. Shrieks and squeals and cries rent the night air.

And then the terrible silence.

★   ★   ★

"Fight-baby-fight. Fight-baby-fight."

I was somewhere so peaceful and so quiet and so comforting, I wanted to stay. I remember aching to go toward a light, a brilliant, welcoming white light ahead of me. And I would have gone, too, I know it. But there was that sound, pulling me back.

"Fight-baby-fight. Fight-baby-fight."

I desperately yearned to get into the glow of that radiance. To bathe in its luminescence. My spirit—I say spirit because I was not conscious of having any form—that spirit that was Cheryl strained toward the brightness. I was almost there. I knew there was serenity in that glow, a peace such as I had never known. And still, the sound would not let me yield.

"FIGHT-BABY-FIGHT. FIGHT-BABY-FIGHT."

It was no use. I could not reach the light. Something was holding me, would not let me go. The brilliance shattered. I opened my eyes and looked into the loving face of my dad.

The most important promise I ever made, was a promise to God and I made it while holding the hand of my step-daughter Cheryl, who was lying near death in a hospital in Tucson. She'd been in a terrible automobile accident and her body was shattered. She was in a deep coma, and the doctors gave her no chance at all. But I wouldn't, I couldn't give up.

So I stayed with her in intensive care. Day after day, holding her hand, talking to her, telling her that I loved her, that we all loved her. The nurses said it was useless, that she couldn't hear me. But I didn't listen.

When Cheryl finally woke up, she told me things I'd said to her. And I spoke to God. I promised God that if he would let her live, I would do something useful with my life, something to make the world a little better because I'd been there.

Cheryl lived and I've tried to keep that promise ever since.

MICHAEL LANDON

I never knew about Michael Landon's promise to God until I read his statement in an interview published not long before he died. I only knew my dad willed me to live nineteen years after I was born.

111

When I regained consciousness in the hospital, the first thing I saw with any clarity was Dad. He was sitting at the end of the bed, holding on to my foot and looking at me. I was shocked that I could see his features so clearly, since I am so very nearsighted. I thought for a moment I must have had my contact lenses in. They weren't. My mother had asked the attendants if I was wearing contacts when they found me after the accident. They'd been removed in the emergency room, so there was nothing to aid my vision. Yet through my eyes, Dad's face was sharply defined, and he was over five feet away. I remember thinking, Wow, this is like a miracle. I can see without my glasses or lenses.

The thought came and went quickly, however, replaced by an intense ache that ran the length and breadth of my body. Instead of going away, the ache grew in intensity and soon established itself as a constant excruciating pain.

I wanted to reach out to Dad, but I couldn't lift my arms. Needles in my arms were attached to tubes connected to all sorts of equipment around my bed. Tubes seemed to be running from every part of my body.

"Oh, Dad," I cried out, "what happened?"

Suddenly Mom was in the room, too. She had stepped out for a moment and Dad had called to her when I revived.

Gently, so very gently, the two of them put their hands on me. We were all crying.

I could not remember what occurred in the immediate aftermath of the accident. My memory began with my arrival at St. Mary's Hospital and with seeing the doctors and nurses bustling around me. I didn't even know how I got there. I buried the memory because the pain of it was too intense, and for the next several years I lived with a hidden pocket of agony locked inside me.

At a future date, the entire episode would come back, replayed in my mind, and I would relive the torment. But for years my unconscious protected me from the ghastly details of that night. My mind censored any recollection of the accident which I am now able to describe.

The attending physician that evening was from India, Dr. Rashid Khan. I learned later that when I was brought in, he looked me over and shook his head. He later said he thought I might have been a pretty girl; he couldn't really tell because I was such a bloody mess. My head had been split open in a straight line from just above my right eye through the eyebrow and forehead and on into my hair-line. I didn't think of it then, of course, but afterward I recalled my visit to the psychic and her parting gesture—she had touched my brow, just where the split occurred.

Dr. Khan operated on me. Dad later was told that some staff members were concerned about my being taken care of by a for-eigner. There was a certain amount of prejudice and the general feeling was I should be in the hands of a good Caucasian doctor. Lucky for me, Dr. Khan was the prime operating physician. That highly skilled and wonderful man put me together again.

Though the incident happened twenty years ago, I can still recall must of the intense emotional agony, if not the physical pain, of the accident. I was in shock and yet my mind was working quite clearly. They had to perform emergency surgery. Among other things, I had a broken bone in my neck, broken ribs, a punctured lung, ruptured spleen, badly crushed and lacerated knees. Not to men-tion the split in my head.

I was prepped for the operating room. A number of doctors and nurses were working over me, and they knew something I wasn't aware of—I was going to be operated on without any anesthesia. I had a concussion and therefore could not be medicated. When they came toward me, I began fighting. I lashed out with my fists and had to be restrained. According to what Dad learned from the police, I had been fighting since the minute I was rescued.

When the police arrived at the accident scene, they found me pinned in the front seat, Dennis's body lying over me. They had to use the jaws of life to cut me out of the wrecked car. For a very long time, I could not remember any of this. Even today, years later and after counseling and therapy, it is still excruciating to recall the terrible, terrifying events that forever changed my life. Now I have remembered, and I will never forget.

At the moment of impact, during those awful grinding, looping turns of the automobile, three of the occupants of that little Volks-wagen were annihilated. Cathy was thrown out and back in through the window and her head was split open. Her date was decapitated. I heard their agonizing screams and saw, out of some corner of my eye, the hellish scene.

In the front seat, Dennis had landed on top of me. I was so wedged into the seat I could not move. I felt the weight of his body. He was moaning softly and breathing heavily, and for what seemed like a long time he lay dying on top of me, and I couldn't say or do anything.

Finally, with a short gasp, he was gone. I felt his body go limp and lifeless. Blood was everywhere, I remember tasting the blood that dripped from his wounds into my face. I felt a fear unlike anything I could ever adequately express. I can only relate it to feeling like a wounded, trapped animal.

For what seemed an eternity, no one came to help. I was alone in the blackness of the night, helplessly trapped with the dead and dying around me.

Then I heard voices. Men talking. They seemed so far away.

"Nobody could be alive in that mess," said one of the voices. I tried to cry out. No sound came from my throat. A beam of light flashed into my eyes. I blinked at the glare.

"My God, there is someone alive in here. Quick! We've got to get this door open."

Dad found out the police had come upon the accident and from the look of the car hadn't expected anyone to have survived. Two of us had; Cathy was still breathing when she was removed from the car. She died in the ambulance on the way to the hospital.

The police got the door off and reached in. They pulled the body off me and when the weight was lifted, I went crazy. I attacked my rescuers and began beating and clawing like a wild animal.

"You were so tough, baby," Dad told me, "you just started fighting for your life."

The doctors said I actually did save my life by all my activity. My broken ribs had pierced a lung, which collapsed. I was hyperventilating and breathing with one lung. I needed to animate myself in order to breathe properly. All the exerted energy supposedly was the reason I survived. Dad couldn't get over my reaction; he just loved the fact that I'd fought.

In the hospital emergency room, after I started punching at the attendants, I was held down as they cut off my clothing. I was wearing jeans and this beautiful floor-length rust-colored knit coat that Mom had bought me. Oh, how I loved that coat; I thought it was so beautiful. Now it was shredded and soaked with blood and being sheared away from my body.

Finally, the clothing had been removed and my battered body was draped with an operating gown. The whole time I moaned and cried, "It hurts, it hurts." One of the doctors leaned over and told me to hold on.

A tube was forced into my chest. I screamed in agony. And then God blessed me and I slipped into unconsciousness.

Once I was identified as Michael Landon's daughter, the authorities went about locating my parents. Dad and Mom were touring and had arrived in Salt Lake City. They were reached at their hotel. Their daughter had been in a terrible car crash, they were informed; the three people with her were dead and Cheryl was not expected to survive.

Dad immediately called the airlines. My parents couldn't get a flight to Tucson quickly enough, so Dad chartered a plane to fly them there. They flew more than two hours not knowing whether they would find me alive or dead.

When my parents arrived at the hospital, I had undergone surgery and was in intensive care. I was still in a coma.

"Look," the doctors told Mom and Dad, "we did all that we could. We have to tell you the chances of her making it are minimal. It would be a miracle if she survived. You better go in and say your good-byes."

Dad and Mom went into the room. Then the two of them settled in for the next few days. They spent most of the day with me, only returning to the hotel late at night.

My father was informed about the accident. He flew into Tucson, went to the hospital that evening and left soon after. I never saw him.

Even though I was in a deep coma, I felt Mom's and Dad's presence. I remember crying out in agony and feeling a soothing cool touch on my head—that was my mother. She was trying to comfort me, and her caress was so loving. Dad was at the foot of the bed and called out to me, "Fight-baby-fight!" No way was my dad going to say good-bye! Truly, he willed me to live.

He was such a powerful person and he used that power for the good of others. I am convinced that I owe him my life.

* * *

The hospital staff didn't believe I had come to. They called me "the Miracle of St. Mary's." I was a pretty battered miracle, I can tell you. I came very close to being paralyzed from breaking a bone in my neck and even closer to being blinded. I'm especially grateful to the doctor for the magnificent job he did of stitching up my face. Really, I'm not self-conscious about the scar because you can barely see it. The rest of my body isn't so great. In fact, I have so many keloids on my back, hands, arms, shoulders, stomach, knees, et cetera, I call myself the Amazon Queen. Others say I have the body of a football player at the end of a long career.

To this day, whenever I wear a bathing suit, people stare at the evidence of my injuries. I'm not embarrassed, though, and in a way I'm kind of proud of what I've gone through. Those scars are tangible evidence of the ordeal. That accident and those surgeries definitely molded me emotionally and spiritually as a person.

I was in a coma for four days. Once I revived, the prognosis improved. The doctors were guardedly optimistic about my recovery. I now had to go about the business of healing.

Mom and Dad were with me constantly. One evening a few days after I'd regained consciousness, they had gone back to the hotel for a well-deserved rest and I was settling in for the night. I was very uncomfortable, and I thought I knew why. I had overheard one of the nurses saying to my mother that I probably would be constipated for a while. I was lying in bed when I felt this terrific pain in my abdomen. I thought the pain would be relieved if I went to the bathroom. I rang for the nurse, but she didn't come.

All of a sudden this unbelievable pain rose inside me, like a volcano erupting. The nurse wasn't there and I simply had to get to the toilet. I dragged myself to my feet and stumbled into the bathroom.

Then I saw my reflection in the medicine-cabinet mirror. I knew it had to be me because no one else was there. I barely recognized myself. I was black and blue and there were huge stitches on my head. My hair had been cut away and I looked as if I'd come back from the dead. And, in fact, I had.

I couldn't look at myself for too long because of the pain. As I sat down on the toilet seat, I suddenly felt dizzy. I began to black out and started to pitch forward. I screamed for help. I saw the floor rushing up toward me and then I passed out. Just at that moment, a cleaning lady came into the bathroom and rushed toward me. I fainted into her arms instead of hitting the floor. If she hadn't been there, I'm certain I'd have cracked my head open on the hard tile.

The cleaning lady called for the nurse and she called for Dr. Khan. He was there in a matter of minutes and examined me. He probed and poked my stomach as gently as possible, but still it hurt terribly.

"Cheryl, dear, we've got to take you into emergency surgery. Your spleen has ruptured."

I don't think I even knew what a spleen was, yet his words struck terror. Tears came into my eyes and I looked at him imploringly.

"Am I going to die?"

"No. You're going to live, Cheryl," Dr. Khan assured me, and I believed him.

The "miracle" of my recovery was continuing. Dr. Khan said if my spleen had ruptured at the same time my lung was pierced, I wouldn't have made it; my body's defensive system would have been on overload. Because I had passed through one crisis, I was able to get through another. Again, the timing had been so important.

My parents were notified and rushed back to the hospital from their hotel. I was taken into the operating room.

The operation went well, and after remaining overnight in recovery, I was returned to my room. Dad and Mom were waiting for me. They looked exhausted. Dad was carrying a sign and he held it up for me to see. It read:

KWITCHERBELLYAKIN.

I put the sign on my hospital bureau and whenever I felt blue or in pain, I'd just look over at it and smile. I couldn't laugh because it hurt too much.

Today, that sign is on the desk in my office.

Word got around that I was in the hospital and lots of people wanted to come and see me. Mom and Dad had made quite a few friends in Tucson, so people started dropping by. One lovely woman brought me religious medals and pinned them to my pillow so that my head was surrounded by 14-karat gold saints. One morning I awoke and found my halo of gold gone.

During the night, someone had come into my room and stolen my medals. The nuns had a fit. They went around the hospital saying that whoever stole the medals was going to Hell.

Unfortunately, they couldn't scare the thief into returning them.

While I was recuperating, Dad took a month off from work to be with me. He was filming some of the last episodes of "Bonanza," which had just about finished its run. Dad was looking for new ventures and had turned down a bunch of inadequate proposals. That's why he went out on the road. He wouldn't take just any job or any movie; he said he'd rather do the rodeos and roll in manure than appear on the screen in anything inferior. Good honest rodeo work was preferable to secondary material. He had a legacy from Little Joe and he didn't want to sacrifice the integrity of his "Bonanza" portrayal.

The pace still was killing. Even with Mom there to pick him up, Dad suffered from exhaustion many times. He had frightening memory lapses, too, when his mind blanked and he couldn't recall recent conversations. Sometimes he couldn't even remember whether he'd eaten or not. Coming to look after me wasn't exactly a respite, but it did slow him down.

Dad and Mom did everything to make the days pass for me as quickly and as easily as possible. While I was recuperating in the hospital, a friend of Dad's brought me a special get-well card. On the front was a photograph from an old gangster movie showing Jimmy Cagney standing between Humphrey Bogart and Frank McHugh. Bogart and McHugh have their guns drawn and pointed toward the camera. Inside the card reads:

If you know what's good for you . . .
you better get well soon!

The card had been autographed by a number of Dad's friends. The signees included Milburn "Doc" Stone from "Gunsmoke," Ralph Bellamy, Jonathan Winters and Jimmy Cagney himself. Down in the lower right-hand corner were two special messages,

I Promised My Dad

Our very best to you
Ronald Reagan

& our prayers
Nancy Reagan

Because of Dad, people were always willing to do special things for his children. One time we went to the NASA Space Center, where I was given a huge poster of the astronauts, which they all signed for me. And among my fondest memories are brief meetings with Elvis Presley and Walt Disney. I kept mementos of these encounters and have a treasure trove of memorabilia, and each item is a precious reminder of a very special occasion.

I remained in St. Mary's Hospital for a month, and for the duration of my stay continued to be known as the Miracle of St. Mary's. The nuns and the nurses told me over and over how fortunate I was, how lucky to be alive.

"You were saved for a special purpose, Cheryl," they told me.

I began to wonder even before I left the hospital why I had been spared and the others taken.

I didn't learn about the fate of my companions until after my own recovery was ensured. When I came out of the coma, one of my first questions was about my friend. "Where's Cathy?" I asked my mother. "Is she okay?"

"She's in the next room, dear," Mom answered. As far as I knew, Cathy was recuperating in the next room, and that's the way it was left until I was strong enough to bear the terrible truth.

As I've said, I had no memory of what had happened. Everything up to my arrival at the hospital was a blank. I could only recall being in the car, and then being in the emergency room.

Mom called the Delta Gamma sisters and kept them up-to-date on my progress. How hard it was on my friends. Cathy's loss was devastating, and for a while, when it looked as though I was a goner, too, absolute dejection descended on the stucco-and-brick sorority house. Mom sent hourly reports by phone to the house as my condition went from critical to guarded. One of the sorority girls became ill herself and was rushed to a local hospital. When Mom heard, she made extra phone calls to the hospitalized girl as well as to the sorority house. I received many cards and calls. So many people were pulling for me.

When I was out of danger and strong enough to bear the news, I was told about the others. I had kept asking my mother about Cathy. "Why isn't Cathy coming to see me? Why can't I talk to her on the phone?" All my questions were answered ambiguously. I accepted the excuses because I didn't see through them. Maybe at the time I didn't want to see through them.

Then, one day, I got really angry that Cathy hadn't come to see me. How dare she! That's when Dad told me what happened to the others.

I didn't cry. I couldn't. The thought that came into my head and stayed there for ever so long was, Why them? Why not me? Cathy was so popular, so bright, such a special person in every way. Why didn't I die with them? Why was I spared? I could find no answers.

I remember that Cathy's sister called me. It was such a lovely gesture, yet all I wanted was to get off the phone. I should have thanked her for calling me, and all I did was end the conversation. I just couldn't handle it. I hope she understood that I was so distraught I didn't know what I was doing.

I remained at St. Mary's through the month of May. Dad and Mom were joined by relatives and friends who dropped by periodically. In early June, my parents took me home. When I was taken down the corridor, one of the doctors walked right past me. He turned around and looked back with his mouth open.

"My goodness. Is that you, Cheryl? I didn't recognize you. I can't believe you're the same person. You look wonderful."

I did, indeed, look wonderful, almost like my old self. Unfortunately, the "look" was deceiving. I may have recuperated physically, but my mind was still a mess. I should have had some sort of therapy. The subject of therapy, however, was never brought up. Psychiatry was the bane of my dad's existence. He'd seen what psychiatry *hadn't* done for his mother, who had been institutionalized at some point. Peggy was in and out of doctors' offices. It became a way of life for her. Consequently, Dad turned his back on a science that might have aided him as well as me. When it came to problems of the mind, he put all his faith in self-help.

I came home from the hospital feeling as strong as a bull. I remember one of the doctors telling me I wouldn't be able to dance anymore, at least not the way I had before. Well, my legs were very built up from all the dancing and I knew I'd be back on the dance floor no matter what the doctor said. And I was. That summer I built myself back up physically. And by the time I was ready to return to school, I thought I could handle anything.

I returned to the sorority house and was greeted with hugs and kisses by all my friends. I felt at home.

The first evening back, we had a rush-week party and the girls sang this song about the accident. The lyrics went on about how Cathy was killed and how they missed her. I'm sure the intentions were of the best, but I was shocked at hearing a ballad about the most hideous moment of my life.

I'm afraid things didn't get much better after that. I assumed everything would be okay once I got back into the swing of school, but I couldn't do it. I had no idea how emotionally blocked I was. I went through the motions and got through a few semesters, but it was only a matter of time before I cracked.

13

*W*ords spoken by a young intern who treated me after my accident have haunted me. "Honey," he said, "when you're through with this, you'll be able to write a book about pain." He was so right! I have endured pain since the accident and will no doubt suffer some form of it for the rest of my life.

At this point, almost twenty years after the accident, I've learned to live with my bodily pain. While my physical wounds were tended to immediately after the crash, the psychological ones were left to fester. In succeeding years there would be subtle changes in my personality, or, if not actual changes, then a heightening of certain characteristics.

I was no longer the pampered darling of Encino and Beverly Hills. I had been through a life-and-death crisis and hadn't yet been able to look at the events squarely. My memory of the accident remained blocked. I went through the motions of a normal life during the day, but in the evenings my subconscious took over and I suffered from nightmares that left me sweating and shaking. Once I awoke to find I had smashed the light next to my bed.

I returned to college, and not long after school started made a trip to Phoenix. I wanted to see the psychic who had predicted the car crash. I'd never forgotten her parting words, "Call me when it happens." I hadn't called her, but I was curious to consult with her again. She'd certainly proved to me she had extrasensory powers.

The psychic was very welcoming and so happy to see me again. I noticed she especially looked at the scar on my forehead.

I asked her if she would tell me things about the future. This time, while there was no trance, she did have shocking news. She held my hand and predicted changes in my family structure. She told me Dad was coming to a divided road in his life and that things looked black. She predicted he would change, and not for the better.

At the time, I put a lot of stock in things like clairvoyance. Then, as I went through various stages of spiritual development, I turned my back on such practices, even destroying all the notes from my meetings with the psychic. Today I look to God as my guide and source of strength. Still, I cannot erase the memory of those prescient things she said about me and my dad. I have to say, despite my doubts about such practices, the woman's forecasts were remarkable.

I wonder sometimes whether, if I had gone to Dad and told him what she had said, would he have changed the course of his actions? Probably not. Even though he himself had moments of psychic awareness, I think he would have found the whole business too threatening.

Because I loved school, I did manage to get through junior year and most of senior year. Things weren't going so well, however. In fact, I was one semester away from being graduated when I quit.

What had happened?

The truth is, I was popping pills like crazy. And I was out of control.

Everything stemmed from that awful car crash. Once you've suffered an injury, you are vulnerable and easily susceptible to further injury. In my junior year, I tore the cartilage in my knee and underwent surgery. The doctor told me I'd never be able to dance again, which, of course, was one of the things I loved most.

After the operation, another blanket of pain was laid over me, pain common to all who suffer severe trauma. I told the doctor about the pain and he prescribed Percodan—*lots* of it. When I went to his office for my regular visits, I received my medication. I learned plenty from those visits.

As I lay in the examination room, I saw other people coming in through the back door of the office. These patients included sports figures whom I recognized. They would just walk in and be handed medicine, and soon I was doing the same thing. In my case, the medication of choice was Percodan. Before long, I was taking six to eight of those babies a day. Fortunately, an observant pharmacist assessed the situation.

He called and asked my dad if he knew I was taking fifty pain pills a week. Dad hit the roof, and was ready to hit the physician who'd prescribed the drug. He phoned the doctor and told him he was through seeing me and threatened to have his license taken away.

The damage was done, however. I was drug-dependent. I believed the pills were the only thing that would help me with the constant pain, the unremitting agony that greeted me in the morning when I awoke and stayed with me until the evening when I went to bed. I know firsthand how dangerous prescribed medicine can be when it is given to the patient without guiding him or educating him to the potential dangers. This reckless practice of administering medicine so casually and carelessly can result in chemical abuse. It certainly did for me. It is equally dangerous to allow a patient to suffer. Proper instruction and monitoring of pain control prevents such abuse.

After Dad and Mom found out about the Percodan use, they became concerned about me being at school, far away from them and any kind of supervision. I had a talk with my dad and he said he thought I should come back to Los Angeles and get a job. He wanted to have me closer to home, where he and Mom could keep an eye on what was happening. The immediate problem was getting me straightened out and off the drug; finishing school and receiving a diploma could be put on hold.

So Dad and Mom set me up in an apartment of my own in the Oakwood Apartments in Burbank. It was one of Mom's rules that you didn't come back home, not after you had set out on your own. I didn't put up a fuss about leaving college, even though I really liked school and would miss my friends. I knew I needed to change my environment. Still, I wish I could have been at home rather than all alone.

With Dad's help I got a job as a page and tour guide at the NBC Studios, which were close by my apartment. I was no longer seeing the doctor who'd prescribed the Percodan. But it didn't matter. In those days, it was very easy to get any substance you wanted. Many people seemed to be taking some drug or other. My family had no idea that, though I'd changed my surroundings, I was still addicted.

One evening I went to a party where I met an old boyfriend of mine from high school. We started talking, and before I knew it, I was talking too much. I was unhappy and this familiar and sympathetic fellow was the perfect audience for my outpouring of woes.

By this time, I'd had it with my job. I was a very good tour guide, and when I started out at NBC I thought I'd be making a lot of new friends and generally having a good time. Well, I wasn't having a good time and I didn't have that many friends because there weren't that many people I could relate to; I was spoiled by the wonderful friends I'd made at college. Furthermore, I was overwhelmed by my new circumstances.

I must have led a pretty sheltered life because I was unprepared for the real world. I was especially surprised at some of the things going on at the studio.

Few there knew I was Michael Landon's daughter, so I was shown no special favors. I was just one of many young people hired to do the lower-level jobs. In order to advance, you had to prove yourself, and there were ways of doing that. Most were legitimate; some weren't. There certainly was one "classic" route for young women to take if they wanted to get ahead.

I remember a seasoned performer coming over to talk to me one day. I told him I hoped to work my way up to production assistant. He smiled and said, "Baby, you're sitting on a million bucks. Why don't you use it?" At first I didn't get what he was saying, then it became all too clear. Over and over again, I saw girls like me being called into the dressing rooms of the stars. They went willingly and they did what they were expected to do. Well, I wouldn't.

I was harassed, too. On one occasion, I was approached by a big star. I was walking outside the studio and this man (who was old enough to be my grandfather) pulled up beside me in his fancy foreign car.

"Get in, honey," he said, pointing to the door, "let's take a little spin." When I said no, he called me a bitch and drove off.

Another time, one of the directors asked me out for dinner. I had a bit of a crush on him and was thrilled that he'd noticed me. Afterward he drove me to his home.

"Okay," he announced, "we've had a great dinner, now we'll have some great sex."

I just looked at him. "That's not what I'm about," I answered, "just take me home."

Grudgingly, he drove me back to my apartment house and complained for the entire trip. He kept telling me he'd never gone out with a woman who hadn't gone to bed with him on the first date.

That's the kind of trashy behavior that occurred. I was disillusioned and disheartened by what I saw. I remember watching Freddie Prinze, the young actor/comedian, take his trip to doom. Prinze was totally stoned out of his mind every single time I saw him. But rather than help the poor guy deal with his obvious problem, they had some caretaker assigned to get him from one place to another. Such was the messed-up world I was involved in and I wasn't ready for it.

My parents didn't realize what was going on. Dad thought it was important for me to start out at the bottom of the ladder and work my way up, as he had done. He was aware of show-biz shenanigans but thought I knew how to protect myself. Once, when I was younger and still wanted to be a dancer, he took me to a soundstage at lunch hour. There had been scads of dancers on the set a few minutes earlier, but not one of them could be seen now.

"You want to be a dancer, baby, I just want you to know what can happen," explained Dad. "If you're wondering where all the dancers are, just check the dressing rooms. They're in there taking care of the guys."

Maybe Dad was exaggerating, but the point had been made. I could see from what went on at the studio that only the tough survive. I was too naive. I just didn't have street smarts. I wish I'd been able to go to my parents and tell them that I was so miserable and lonely, but I couldn't. I was too ashamed. When I was with them, I tried to act as though everything were okay, but the truth was, I was falling apart even as I desperately tried to hold myself together. The only thing that kept me going was the pills, or so I thought.

After the knee surgery, I went back and forth to doctors and physical therapists. I told them I was in terrible pain from the surgery and they tried to help me. One evening I went to an emergency room for relief. A doctor walked in, looked me over and analyzed the situation.

"Do you need help?" he asked.

I looked at his kind face, and answered, "Yes."

I admitted myself to the hospital. Later, the tabloids and magazines got hold of the story and really blew it out of proportion. They made it sound as though I had been a hard drug addict for years and had been going in and out of rehab centers. I learned early on how dangerous it is to be ill when you're in the public eye. If you're sick, those magazines and papers will make you sicker.

Dad and Mom came to see me in the hospital. I remember being glad I was out of that lonely apartment, even if I was in a hospital bed.

I have to say the treatment wasn't that effective. The hospital thought that Thorazine was the answer. It wasn't. I could con my way around most of the staff. After a few weeks I was released and returned to my apartment in Burbank and my job at NBC. The explosion would come eventually. It was inevitable. It was only a matter of time.

Much has been written about the prevalence of drugs in the everyday life of the seventies, especially in cities like Los Angeles. I want to say, however, that while drug use may have been widespread, it was never part of my life at home. I knew kids who came out of families where they got stoned together; that never happened at our house. Drugs weren't tolerated.

I became a substance abuser, but I didn't consciously equate taking Percodan with drug abuse. After all, the pills were being prescribed by a doctor, and for the singular purpose of helping to dull my pain.

I began amassing pills. When I had run through all the prescription drugs I could get, I started to steal them. I'd go to people's houses and head right for the bathroom. I'd check the medicine cabinets and take what I wanted. I built up an arsenal of pills.

Ever since the doctor told me I wouldn't be able to dance again, I'd load up on painkillers, then go out to discos and dance my feet off, just to prove him wrong. One evening I went to a private club in Beverly Hills called Pips. I'd scheduled a movie date for that evening with a guy I'd been in love with once upon a time. We'd broken up when I went to college, but when I came back, we found each other again. He had called earlier in the evening, apologizing for having to break the date, and saying that he had to go out of town for the evening. We made arrangements to get together the next night. Since I was all set to step out, I decided to go to Pips on my own.

When I got there, I had the supreme pleasure of seeing my boyfriend on the dance floor with another girl. He'd broken our date and gone out with someone else. I'm sure he didn't expect to see me there, since we were supposed to go to the movies. However, when he did catch sight of me, he didn't blink an eye. He ignored me and continued to dance with his date. He began kissing her, too, and he knew damn well I was there. He'd looked straight at me. I was humiliated and infuriated.

Blinded by fury, dizzy with pain, and dazed with drugs, I went on a real self-destructive binge.

I ran home, raided my medicine cabinet, and began popping pills. I spent the evening stuffing myself with poison.

I couldn't bear to be alone and I didn't dare to go to my parents. I felt I had no one to talk to, not even Dad. He was tough on drug abuse. He felt that there was no excuse for it. Sure, he'd been addicted himself in those years before he met Mom and had described in detail how the drugs and drinking had dragged him down till he felt like a "marshmallow," but he had picked himself up by his bootstraps and gone cold turkey. His unyielding attitude on this subject was that since he had done it, so could everyone. Plus he didn't believe that you needed therapy or special help. In fact, you couldn't bring up the subject of psychiatry with him; it was one of his few real blind spots. As far as Dad was concerned, his mother was proof of the inadequacy of psychiatric care. He felt you should be able to just say no, and that was that.

I felt so low, so unbelievably low. I began to think of taking so many pills I'd pass out. I wanted to cut everything out. I wanted to cut myself out. In plain English, I was suicidal.

In my foggy state I decided to leave the apartment and move in with Ginny Jean and Granddad. I grabbed a suitcase, threw in some clothes, and then took every pill I could put my hands on and dumped them in too.

On the way over to my grandparents' house the same horrible thoughts I'd been having for nearly two years tormented me. Everything boiled down to the car crash and the burden of being the one who'd miraculously escaped death.

I carried on a dialogue in my mind, proclaiming the unfairness: "You survived that crash. You lived and those boys and Cathy died. You were saved for this wonderful mission. What mission? To be constantly in pain and medicated out of your mind? You don't deserve to live! And you don't even have the guts to cut your wrists!"

By the time I reached my grandparents' I was a shaking wreck.

I walked in the front door and tried to pretend I was just dropping by for a visit. My uncle Bob, Mom's brother, was there with his girlfriend. He took one look at me and realized I was bombed out of my mind. He took the suitcase from me and opened it.

"Oh, my God!" he cried when he saw all the stuff. He went to the phone and called my parents. Dad must have said to throw the drugs out because Bob called out to his girlfriend to unpack the suitcase and ditch the contents. I began crying and tried to stop her. Bob was standing in front of me, with a huge window behind him. I leapt past my uncle and dashed toward the window. I wanted to crash through; I wanted to slash myself, to cut myself up, to stop the pain.

My uncle caught me and pulled me back. I struggled to get free, then collapsed in tears.

Dad rushed over to get me. I was sitting doubled over when he walked in. Without saying a word, he sat down opposite me and lifted his arms toward me. I stood up and went over to him. Gently, he drew me onto his lap just as he had when I was a little girl. He put his arms around me and held me close. He was crying and so was I.

We cried together and then he cupped my face in his hands and drew my head away so that he could look at me. He shook his head slowly and said in a choked voice, "You're an addict, baby, a damn addict, and you need help."

14

Do you remember the episode in "Little House on the Prairie" when Pa Ingalls had to take his daughter Mary to a school for the blind? The Ingallses had done everything for Mary at home until it became obvious they had done all they could. Mary needed special attention in order for her to improve further, to be at her best, in order for her to realize her potential. Pa Ingalls said his good-byes knowing that a long, long time would pass before he'd see his beloved child again. The farewell between parent and child was very moving, so moving that television viewers all across America were reduced to tears. Lots of letters were written to the studio about that episode, and all of them mentioned how real and how moving the program was.

That particular show was a perfect example of Dad's incredible gift for distilling his real-life experiences and pouring them into his work. It came from the ordeal he went through with me. Actually, I'd say about ninety-nine percent of our family situations wound up on Dad's shows, which probably was why they appealed to audiences so much. They were grounded in reality.

I wasn't physically blind like Mary Ingalls, but I was blind to my own condition. I simply had no sense of what was wrong with me, and my family had done all they could. A time came when I had to

131

say good-bye to Dad and Mom, to my sisters and brothers, to my grandmother and all the relatives and friends I loved so dearly. I had to leave them and go to a place where I could straighten myself out.

I was twenty-two years old, and as my dad had said, I was an addict. Now something had to be done. In cases like mine, most people would enter a rehabilitation center or hospital for professional medical help. Because of his aversion to the traditional psychiatric methods which he believed had not helped his mother's life, Dad didn't want me in a psychiatric setting. Mom felt different, considering psychiatry a very helpful tool, but she yielded. She didn't buck Dad because she knew how strongly he felt on the subject. (Later, when Mom and he were separating, my mother sought help from a psychiatrist for a short time. She pleaded with Dad to join her or to see someone on his own. He refused.)

My parents began to look for the right place for me. There had to be some environment where people like me could be helped. After all, I was not the only young woman with a problem; there were many, many, many of us.

"You can do the best you can for your kids," Dad explained to an interviewer, "and they can do the best for you, but it's not always what's right."

Mom and Dad talked to their friends about me. They were concerned and upset, and they found relief in discussing the matter with intimates. Additionally, they hoped someone might come up with a valuable suggestion. As it turned out, one did.

Dad's business manager told him he had friends whose children had suffered major problems including drug abuse. A few of these troubled kids had gone to CEDU, a residence facility founded in 1967 in Running Springs, California, in the San Bernardino National Forest. These kids had come out clean and gone on to finish college or get on with their lives in a productive manner. CEDU was available to anyone who exhibited any form of anti-social or self-destructive behavior, from drug use to arson to attempts at suicide. CEDU is pretty much what it says, "See" yourself as you are, and "Do" something to change. "See-do," or CEDU.

Mom and Dad arranged to meet with some of the kids who'd been there and what they heard made them eager to get me into the program. The graduates were quite enthusiastic; some were actively working to raise money for the center. All of them said CEDU had been the best experience of their lives, indeed, had *saved* their lives.

Dad and Mom did further investigating. They found out that CEDU was not a medical facility, but a school with a structured and disciplined curriculum. The program was run by educators and by the students themselves. Though there was a nurse on duty, the emphasis was on getting better through good honest effort rather than relying on medication and doctors. This "tough love" approach appealed to Dad.

Dad spoke to the CEDU people and explained the situation. He told them I'd started taking pills to kill the pain from the injuries I'd sustained in the car accident, but that it had become apparent I'd moved on to another level of drug use.

"Eventually, the physical pain is only an excuse to take the drugs," he said in an interview. "I'm not saying all pain pills should be abandoned. And heaven knows we were blessed with doctors whose skills saved Cheryl's life. But along the way, there can always be one doctor who over-prescribes."

Dad and Mom were impressed that CEDU residents learned to function without relying on medication, to live without crutches like the painkillers. The important thing was that eventually you learned you *could* live *without* them if you didn't absolutely need them, or you could live *with* them, sensibly, if you did.

Dad and Mom were sold. They put their faith in CEDU and thank God for that.

"We hoped to hell you had the guts we thought you had to stick it out," Dad later told me.

After Mom and Dad decided I should go to CEDU, they told the other kids, or at least they told Leslie, who was thirteen, and Michael, who was eleven; Shawna and Christopher were four and one, too young to understand.

It was really hard for Leslie and Michael to deal with the fact that their big sister had big problems. Sure, they'd seen my mood swings and had witnessed my erratic behavior, but they had no comprehension of the extent of my illness. As Dad put it, "There are thousands of parents trying to pretend that what's wrong with their children is just a phase they're going through. In some cases, they don't want to admit it. But you have to—you have to face the truth."

Well, we faced the truth.

★   ★   ★

I have to say that Dad and Mom didn't force me to go. There was an implicit suggestion that I do something for myself and CEDU was offered as the best of choices. One of the things that scared me was the length of the program. Going there meant committing myself to a stay of no less than eighteen months to two years. It seemed such a long time to be away from my family. Yet I realized I really wasn't *with* my family as I was now. I had reached the point where I couldn't do it on my own. Here was an opportunity to join others like me, to fight back and become a responsible and independent person.

One morning my parents suggested we drive up and take a look at the place. If it seemed right, I could make my decision to stay when we got there. Just in case, I packed my suitcase—I had a feeling I would be needing it.

CEDU is situated in the midst of a pine forest with breathtaking views of the San Bernardino Valley. The site was lovely, and didn't look at all institutional. I decided I wanted to give the place a try; given my circumstances, it was the only decision I could make. Besides, I wasn't going to be a prisoner there; I could leave anytime.

Saying good-bye to Dad and Mom was really hard. I hugged and kissed them both, and then they were gone. Dad later said as difficult as it was to leave me, it was a relief to lie in bed at night and know he wouldn't be getting a 3 A.M. phone call saying, "Your daughter's OD'd."

Now I was alone, or so I felt at first. As I soon learned, I was not really alone—I was among my peers, brothers and sisters joined in a common fight.

CEDU came on strong. You had to be stripped of all your false defenses as well as your pills. Vanity went out the window. Almost the first thing they did was cut my hair. Like Dad, I wore it long, very long, and, like him, I had strong feelings about the length. At CEDU, it didn't matter.

There were about one hundred and twenty students at CEDU and twenty staff members, including teaching interns who came from nearby colleges. The staff was warm, loving, and tough. Some were former CEDU students.

Living arrangements were set up to integrate us into the community and then to move us forward into more independent states.

Everyone began in the Genesis group, the beginning. During the initial part of our stay, we were under the closest supervision. We slept in dormitories with four to a room.

Those first months at CEDU were tough. When I wrote to my parents, I pretended everything was fine. I made jokes about the work schedule and things like having my hair shorn and my makeup confiscated. I tried to pretend to them I was thrilled with getting down to basics. I wasn't, of course—I was unhappy and I was terrified. I know they saw through my bluff. After a while, I was able to be more honest about the situation, and I wrote and told them about the difficulties I was facing. Eventually I was again writing letters about how good things were, but this time I wasn't pretending.

Mom and Dad came to visit me as often as they could. Sometimes they brought others, like Leslie and Michael, or Uncle Bob, or Ginny Jean and Granddad. I loved their visits, especially when they'd take me out to lunch in town.

Once I was out of the Genesis group, I was allowed to go home and visit. At first I was accompanied by a teacher. Then I could go home on overnight passes. Dad told me that it was such a thrill to see me. He said I had changed so in my appearance and demeanor: I was no longer withdrawn and tense. He told me I looked like a kid again. "You're beautiful, baby, and you're with it again," he said proudly.

I really was getting it together again, and I was so enthusiastic about CEDU that I wanted to share it with my family. I told them all about my life there. I told them so much, in fact, that I expect they felt they had been through the CEDU experience as well.

CEDU operates on a strict work ethic. While you're there, you have to pull your weight, you have to work. There were rules at CEDU, and if you didn't follow them, if you shirked your work, you had to make it up.

I became very involved with the CEDU community and I wanted to help keep it going. I started busing and waiting tables in the dining room. Then, I became the baker.

After leaving the dormitory, I moved into a cabin and worked at the White House, CEDU's business office. There were about thirty of us in the group, and while the kids were great, I had real problems with the head of the family. He seemed to have it in for me for some reason. I became so unhappy that I might have left if Brenda Kimble hadn't intervened. Brenda, who was managing the office at the time, is a great and wonderful lady and remains my friend to this day. She recognized that I was having trouble; moreover, she saw it was through no fault of mine. The man was just gunning for me. Perhaps it was the old "Let's get the daughter of the celebrity" syndrome in operation again.

When Mel Wasserman, founding director of CEDU, was advised of my dilemma, he took over my case and I worked directly with him.

At the White House, I was fund-raiser for CEDU. Phone duty can be very discouraging; you have to learn how to take rejection. It's the same kind of thing my dad went through when he was a salesman. He learned how to roll with the punches, and so did I.

Having been successful at fund-raising, my second year I began teaching a drama workshop. I directed one production, appeared in a few others, and actually became part of the teaching staff.

While at CEDU, I continued my studies for my bachelor's degree. Giving the drama class at CEDU had sparked my interest in teaching. I decided I wanted to make it my career.

15

At CEDU I had a lot of time to think about my life, especially about what had happened to me since the auto accident. I started to look for reasons rather than excuses for my behavior. Finally I began to face my problems instead of running away from them. The one thing that become so apparent was that everything led back to the accident.

After the fatal crash, after I had been dubbed the Miracle of St. Mary's, after I had been told over and over again how lucky I was to have survived and how God had a "purpose" in letting me live, after I tried desperately to find my mission in life, after all that—I found I could not face living. Instead I began to self-destruct.

It was a slow process. On the surface I seemed to be doing okay, but underneath there was a steady gnawing away at my spirit. I repressed so much, an explosion was inevitable.

In the months following the auto accident I had become a "celebrity" in my own right—I was the girl who miraculously had escaped death. There had to be a reason for my survival; I must be, in some way, blessed.

Everyone who spoke to me about the accident did so with the best of intentions. Yes, I was lucky. Yes, God must have had a plan.

Yes, there must have been a reason. And yet I could not find one. I was so glad to be alive, but I couldn't express my joy. I could not deal with the burden of survival. I felt unworthy from the moment I heard I was the only one to come out of the car crash. I didn't know the two boys very well, but I did know Cathy and she was a far better person than I ever could be, or so I believed. She had died, I had lived. *Why?*

Since the accident, I had been carrying the burden of "why" and no one knew it, not even I myself. No one could reach me, not even my dad, despite how hard he tried.

Unless you've been in a similar experience yourself, you have no idea of the torture involved in being a survivor. How miserable you feel as you smile and say, "Yes, I'm glad to be alive," while inside you never stop wondering *why you are*. What is it you have to be glad about, since your life is tied up with the deaths of others? And, equally petrifying, because you beat the odds, people begin to believe that you might be blessed in a special way, a way that could help others. Suddenly, you are asked to perform miracles. A short time after my automobile accident, such a request was made of me.

The beloved seventeen-year-old son of good friends of our family had been struck by a car and lay in a coma in Cedars-Sinai Medical Center. He was a wonderful kid, and I loved him as I loved my brothers. According to the doctors there was nothing to be done; he was far too severely injured to pull through. It was only a matter of time, they said. That's when his mother called me.

"Please, Cheryl," she begged, "come into the room with him. Touch him, hold his hand, anything. You came back, you did it. Maybe you can bring him back. Please help him!"

She was grasping at any straw. She was so crazed with grief, she wanted me to perform a miracle. A miracle from the miracle girl. I was terrified. I had no powers; my own life was a shambles. What could I do? I didn't want to go, and yet, how could I refuse?

I went to the hospital and sat by my friend's bed. I put my hand over his, leaned over his still body, and said words like the words Dad had said to me. I tried so hard, so very, very hard.

Nothing changed.

I kept on living. That splendid, beautiful boy died.

I had failed him, I had failed his parents. To me, here was

another example of my unworthiness, another example of my throwing away the gift of life that had been bestowed upon me. This was what I had to live with, the knowledge that I had been saved for nothing.

At the same time the auto accident shattered my physical and emotional being, it shaped and formed me. My adult life began with that crash, but emotionally I was unprepared. The only way I could deal with the shock and terror was to repress it.

For two years, I lived with the shadow of death hanging over me, the memory of the accident buried in my subconscious, coming forward only in dreams, nightmares that haunted me and hurled me into despair. Along with the constant pain, those hideous dreams became my legacy—until I came to CEDU. Not only did CEDU help me regain myself, it also was the place where I, at last, was able to face my demons.

One afternoon, during a session with Mel Wasserman, I was led into a state of self-hypnosis during which I fully recalled the automobile accident.

I remembered everything. The shock of the collision. Being hurled through the night and turning over and over. Hearing the crunch and screech of the metal along the ground and the disembodied screams of terror coming from my own throat as well as from the others. Seeing those others lying mutilated and annihilated, being trapped under the dying body of my date, the blood, the carnage, and the torment—it all came back to me and I relived every awful moment.

As I went through the whole hideous incident again, Mel allowed me to do all the screaming and crying I had repressed for so long. When I came out of my hypnotic state with the full memory of the accident from start to finish, I was shaken. At the same time I experienced a feeling of utter relief.

Mel talked to me for a bit and then said, "Why don't you go and take a walk by yourself, Cheryl; it'll do you good."

I'll never forget that stroll through the beautiful forests of San Bernardino. I walked among those giant trees and cried and cried and cried. I cried for so many things. I cried for the little girl who'd had no real home and no real father or mother for so long. I cried for the terrible things I had done to myself. I cried for those poor souls, Cathy, Dennis, and Mike, who had died. Most of all, I cried because I was so thankful to be alive.

This was the first time I could fully express my gratitude; the first time I dared to be glad that I had been spared; the first time I could allow myself to rejoice in my being alive.

16

My CEDU experience not only freed me from an unhealthy life-style and insufferable guilt, it also allowed me to go back and address my earlier problems of abandonment. I learned how to deal with my feelings toward my biological father and to embrace fully the man I loved and honored as my dad.

In all the years Michael Landon had acted as my parent, supporting me emotionally as well as materially, I had to call him Mike. I ached to call him Dad, but my father had forbidden me to do so.

"I'm your father," he'd sternly interject whenever I'd slip and refer to Mike familiarly, "I'm the one who gave you life."

For almost two decades, I'd honored my father's demand out of fear and a certain kind of respect. After all, he *was* my father and I didn't want to insult him even though I didn't think that calling Mike "Dad" was such a terrible thing. That's when Dad was so understanding and so reassuring. "It doesn't matter what you call me, I'm your dad," he'd say whenever there was a flare-up. "Always remember, Cheryl, you are my daughter."

Certainly I always felt like his daughter. Why wouldn't I? Everything he did made me feel secure in his love, from his close attention and supervision to his taking over all my financial needs. It was Dad who paid the entire bill for my hospitalization and recuperation after the car crash. There was no insurance, either. And he never once made any mention of his generosity. He took care of everything and never threw it in my face. He never said, "Boy, you cost me a lot of money." I was never "Lynn's child"; I was his child, and he was responsible for me—it was as simple as that.

My own father tried in his way to be a good father, but he didn't understand my needs as a daughter. He demanded singular devotion, and when I tried to give it to him, he spurned me. He ranted and raged against Michael Landon and bitterly complained about the awkward position he'd been put into as a "non"-father. I took everything personally. I felt it was my fault. One time, there was a squabble over my being in a newspaper article about the Landons. I burst into tears and stood there sobbing. Why was he yelling at me? I didn't print the article. I can see him now, as he sat there watching me cry my heart out without offering any kind of comfort. He just stared at me and at the end said curtly, "It's your problem."

If only he'd tried to meet me halfway, we might have been able to forge some kind of healthy relationship. I never wanted to make a choice between him and Dad. Though I tried to be a daughter to both of them, I couldn't satisfy my father's insatiable and unreasonable demands for exclusivity. And yet, despite everything, I still loved him.

CEDU helped me to find the courage and freedom to make my own choices. I *wanted* to call Michael Landon my father, and I did. I came home from CEDU and Dad and Mom and I stood together in a circle and cried and embraced. Dad was beaming, he was so proud of my new confidence.

"Gosh, look how she carries on conversations," he told Mom. "She's funny and she's lively. She's Cheryl again."

I *was* Cheryl again. I was full of moxie. The day I left CEDU, I began to call Michael Landon Dad, and that's what I called him to the day he died. I will always call him Dad.

Alas, just about the time I began calling him Dad, he was beginning to move away, if not from his children, then certainly from his wife, my mother.

For so many years Dad and Mom had been the perfect couple, and I believe they truly were. Their union seemed invincible. True, their original ardor, the all-consuming need for Dad to have Mom with him, had waned. After seventeen years, it wasn't surprising. If Romeo and Juliet had lived to marry and grow old together, they probably wouldn't have been doing balcony scenes in their forties.

To me, and to most others, the shift in my parents' relationship seemed more of an adjustment than a cooling. Dad really wasn't traveling anymore; the rodeo- and club-circuit days had passed. He had become an executive, a producer-director-writer-actor rather than a touring artist. He spent his days at the studio or on location while Mom was busy at home raising Leslie, Michael, Jr., Shawna, and then, Christopher.

Interestingly, though both my parents adored having children, at one point they decided to stop. Not long after Michael, Jr., was born, Mom had a serious miscarriage, one that required hospitalization. As a result, Dad had a vasectomy. A couple of years later, while on vacation, they saw a particularly beautiful baby. "Are you sorry we didn't have more kids?" Dad asked. She was, and so he had the vasectomy reversed, at the time a very difficult procedure. I'm sure glad they did, because Shawna and Christopher came along. Like Leslie and Michael, Jr., they're not just brothers and sisters I love because of blood ties, they're truly fabulous people.

I remember when Mom told me she was expecting, months before Chris was born. She was giggling and seemed even a little embarrassed. "Oh, my gosh, Cheryl, I can't believe it. I'm pregnant," she said.

I thought it was terrific, although I couldn't help thinking that in the usual run of things *I*, at my age, would more likely have been making such an announcement. It was a real role reversal. Mother's last pregnancy came after the family had moved to Beverly Hills.

When we made that move, there was a shift in values as well as in our way of life. Despite his good intentions, Dad was sowing the seeds of the destruction of his marriage by overindulging us. And, the more we had, the more he seemed to resent our luxurious life. He said it was his error and not our fault. Still he was dissatisfied and working all the time. The harder he worked, the less time he had to spend at home. In a way, Dad had two families, ours, and one on whatever television show he was working on.

Dad always had made it a rule to close his set at six o'clock so everyone could get home for dinner. He created an empire on the television soundstage, and he ruled there. Mom reigned over the

Beverly Hills estate. Two separate kingdoms existed. Mom had less and less to do with Dad's work and I think it took away from her identity. Mom had been a comrade for Dad for so long; now she was turning into a fashionable housewife.

It was a far cry from their early days. In the beginning Mom felt secure with Dad and he relied on her. She was his constant companion. If Dad said, "Come with me," she never hesitated. And those trips usually weren't to glamorous resorts, either. The typical destination was a place like the Cornstalk Inn somewhere in Iowa, hardly a watering spot for trendy jet-setters.

But it didn't matter to them. Wherever they went, they had fun together. There was a dignity in their alliance that Dad wouldn't compromise. Mom was aware that other women were after him, but he never let them near him. Whenever he was approached by ardent females, he'd politely brush them off, saying, "I only kiss children and old ladies."

Dad recognized the temptations, but he respected Mom too much to yield to them. He admitted being a jealous person himself and said it was better for him to have his wife around. "She makes everything bearable," he told a reporter, adding that whatever happened, he and Mom could always go back to their hotel room and have a "cheeseburger and a chuckle."

A "cheeseburger and a chuckle"—that was my parents' story in a nutshell—it speaks of the closeness, the simplicity, and the fun. They laughed a lot together, Mom and Dad. There's no doubt she was the best thing that ever happened to him. She helped him beat the habits that had been destroying him and she inspired him to use his most creative forces.

Dad said of his writing and directing career, "I didn't have a lot of motivation, but when I met Lynn, I found I had someone who believed in me, who was supportive of me. I wanted her to be proud of me. If I hadn't met her, I don't think I would have done any of this."

Mom and Dad talked together all the time. He presented his concepts to her and occasionally she gave ideas to him, ideas that really paid off.

For instance, one of Mom's favorite movies was *The Bishop's Wife*. In the film, Cary Grant plays an angel who comes to earth to help people out. Among other good deeds, he makes it possible for the bishop, David Niven, and his wife, Loretta Young, to raise money for a new church. Mom was crazy about the movie, and so were the rest of us; viewing it became an annual Christmas holiday ritual.

When Dad was searching for a new series after he and Mother had split and "Little House on the Prairie" was ending, he came up with a project called "Highway to Heaven." Remember the premise of "Highway to Heaven"? About an angel who comes to earth to help out people? The truth is that Mom told Dad this theme would make a good series.

Dad had been a doting husband, sometimes going even beyond doting. He never wanted Mom out of his sight. Over and over, he demonstarted his great need for her. I remember one time when Mom went with me to San Francisco. Dad decided to fly up from Los Angeles to surprise her. On his way to the airport, his car broke down. What did he do? He hailed a passing truck, which picked him up and drove him to the airport. The truck was used to deliver pianos and Dad sat in the back with all the merchandise. He did it just because he wanted to be with Mom. It seemed he'd go to any extreme sometimes just to be at her side.

If Mom had any complaints about Dad, they had to do with his obsession with work and its effects on him. She worried about his health. Although he was a loving father, Mom thought he often acted more like one of us kids than the head of the household. In general, Mom was right, but I loved that childlike quality in my dad. I think the reason he behaved as he did—playful, like a little boy—had to do with his own miserable early years. He had missed the fun of childhood then, but he could enjoy at least a small part of it now.

Mom didn't shirk her duty. She ran a tight ship, or at least she tried to.

Though I rarely saw Dad lose his temper, I did see him begin to sink into black moods. At the end of his marriage to Mom, he began to suffer real depressions. We experienced the "tip" of those depressions before the breakup; they went much deeper after he had gone.

17

When I first graduated from CEDU, I moved to San Francisco where I lived for a time with my dear uncle Bob and worked for a title-insurance company. I started out as a desk clerk and moved my way up to escrow secretary. Thanks to CEDU, I was able to work much better now, was more equipped mentally and emotionally to compete in the workplace. Now I was slugging it out in the real world, holding my own, not trying to play off my looks or material possessions. It was fun; it was challenging.

The last course I needed to fulfill my formal college-degree requirement was geology, which I completed through a correspondence course. Then, in San Francisco, I attended the state university to do graduate work. Believe it or not, I had to leave after one semester because the campus was so unsafe. Crime was rampant and many instances of rape were reported; you needed partners to walk with you at night. I transferred to the College of Notre Dame in Belmont, a school run by nuns. It was there I finished my fifth year of advanced education and got my teaching credentials.

I was on solid ground at last. My happy scenario had only one flaw, and it was a major one—the growing rift between my parents.

★   ★   ★

147

I saw Mom and Dad's relationship had changed a few years after the move to Beverly Hills, during the seventeenth year of their marriage. I never saw them fight, but when I came home from school, I sensed something was in the air. "You really should talk to your mother," Dad once told me angrily, "she's got some crazy ideas. I don't know what's got into her."

Another time, he pulled me aside and said, "You've got to talk to your mom. She's behaving so strangely."

In fact, Mom wasn't behaving strangely—he was! And he was trying to shift the responsibility onto her. He was caught up in living a lie. The man who demanded honesty from others was dealing in deceit.

The truth is, Dad was involved with a woman half his age, a woman a few years younger even than I.

He first saw her on the set of "Little House on the Prairie," and she had her eye on him, too. Dad, who had been so enamored of his wife that he only "kissed children and old ladies"; Dad, who had been the ideal husband for so many years and whose family life meant everything in the world to him; Dad, who had been the symbol of patriarchal integrity for millions of television viewers as well as his own family—that Dad had strayed.

When my family moved to Beverly Hills, Mom described her life there as if she were living in a fantasy world and not reality. Dad was in control. He never wanted her to work and set up Mom's life to be as carefree as possible, with shopping, lunches and playing tennis with friends. Sometimes Mom would even see Dad parked across the street, checking up on her. Eventually, this lifestyle itself created problems, destroying Mom and Dad's marriage as their values started changing. Like so many celebrity couples, their priorities became confused, and my parents lost sight of what was really important. "Only," Mom says, "you don't notice these things and their repercussions at the time."

Dad always said he wanted to keep things simple; yet he himself put us into the grand social mainstream, where life became unrealistic and the distancing between us began. This was the man who always thought of himself as a kind of frontier character, no fuss or frills. He called himself "the Jewish Cowboy," and referred to our family group as the "the Jewish Cowboy and his Goyim."

Dad and Mom didn't like fancy dinners or balls or anything like that. Though he'd go to hospitals and homes anywhere and at any time to visit the sick and the dying, he loathed getting all "duded up" to attend elaborate affairs. They loved simple gatherings and such high society events were not their idea of fun.

We weren't in Encino and our new way of life was very different, certainly more sophisticated. Dad still wanted to think of himself as a simple cowboy, but he wasn't. Ours wasn't a cowboy's home; it was a rich man's mansion and we were a rich and famous man's family. If anything, he was a "Beverly Hills Cowboy." We went from being an easygoing, typical American family to living the life of the rich and famous. And it affected even the most rudimentary things, like meals.

In Encino, things were more casual. Sometimes Dad would do the cooking. And there were those wonderful alfresco dinners in the carport when the air conditioner broke down. Now we had a more formal dining room with correct napery and appointments, and servants prepared and served the food and Mom rang the bell for dinner.

Mother was the chatelaine and had a sense of her responsibilities. She rose to the occasions Dad tried to ignore. She adjusted. She adapted. She couldn't rattle around in this palace the same way she had in our Encino home. The funny thing is, Dad became unhappy with the way Mother was acting. He thought she got too caught up with being a Beverly Hills matron. What else could she have done? She *was* a Beverly Hills matron, a responsible adult who took her role seriously.

First came her children. She watched over my brothers and sisters and taught all of us to behave like ladies and gentlemen. She had a gracious air and a great sense of style, from both of which Dad benefited as well. She picked out his clothes and helped him in his dealings with others. She was very good at handling touchy situations. If someone stepped out of line, Mom always had the right words, and they were never crude. Mom is a lady.

Dad relied on her social graces. He was able to focus on his work, knowing she would help him with everything else. It's funny, too, because Mom, like Dad, was basically shy. After she married Dad and gave up modeling, she never wanted to be in the limelight again. Dad was the performer. Sometimes, though, Dad would bring her onto some show or other. She was particularly terrified of doing talk shows and Dad, of course, was in demand. His bright repartee and his charming manner were real assets for any program.

One time in the late 1960s, Dad got Mom to go with him on "The Mike Douglas Show." She stood in the wings waiting for her cue to enter and was almost frozen with fear.

Dad was standing with Mike Douglas and said casually that he'd like Mike to meet his wife. "And," says Dad, "here she is, my wife, Lynn." He motioned toward Mom and she walked zombie-like onto the set. She went up to Mike Douglas and Dad, shook *Dad's* hand, mumbled, "Nice to meet you," then turned around and walked away.

Those were the days when my dad just *had* to have her with him no matter where he went. She was his drug. In the first decade of their marriage, Dad's passionate attachment was smothering. Mom later recognized that the intensity of his feeling really manipulated her responses. She couldn't bring herself to upset his love because he became so unhinged. Remember, this was a man who was hiding in automobiles to see if she really was at a knitting class!

In varying degrees, Dad was passionate about all of the people he loved. In his desire to envelop us with devotion, there's no question he spoiled all of us tremendously. And when he'd finished and didn't like what he saw—"the Beverly Hills family" for example— instead of dealing with it, he'd left. Because we all were so intoxicated by this man's unconditional love, because he could love you like no one else in the world, his abrupt departure was catastrophic. Suddenly everything became frightening.

As the oldest child, I became Dad's sounding board. He voiced his complaints and concerns to me. I listened to his reasons and told him I thought he was making a mistake. He was treating my mother dreadfully. Perhaps because I was the oldest, or because I had this special bond with Dad, I was able to remain neutral, at least on the surface. Believe me, I wasn't feeling neutral inside. I was seething. I just couldn't believe Dad could be so cruel to Mom and to us.

Though she never mentioned it to us, my mother knew, or at least suspected, that he was carrying on an affair. Dad went away on fishing trips that Mother found "fishy." She began to say things and Dad got very touchy. But instead of talking to her, he spoke to me. He didn't talk to the other kids about this, I think, because they were too young. He talked to me because he realized I was his only potential ally.

My siblings had grown up in a house of love; I'd been the one plucked out of an unhappy state. I was a lost and confused child when this total stranger gave me the compassion and care I craved. He treated me with honest affection and molded me into a product that reminded him a lot of himself. My debt to him went beyond those of his natural children.

At the time I did not really understand temptation. Dad was depressed and confused. He never stood a chance against a younger woman. She was after him and the timing was perfect. He was only human. I didn't want to blame him; I wanted to blame the circumstances.

Looking back, I wish I had spoken up more but Dad's happiness was important to me. When I went through my dark stages, Dad stuck by me. When he went through his crisis, I did the best I could. I didn't want to antagonize him. I just kept praying he'd "wake up." I held on to the memory of the wonderful years we had shared together, always hoping they could be recaptured.

While the predominate feeling was one of estrangement, there were moments when we were able to enjoy some of the warmth of bygone days. Though those times became fewer and farther between, they were very precious to me because they indicated that some trace of the Dad I knew remained. I'd had his guidance and presence during my adolescence and teens, and that was important.

Then suddenly he was gone, no longer a part of the world I had known for so long, no longer a part of the home I could go to for comfort. And so for the next few years it seemed I stood by the wayside and grabbed whatever crumb of attention or affection I could get from him.

It was very difficult to accept his betrayal. My biggest role model in the whole wide world had walked away, turned his back on all of us. In a way, it would have been easier to accept his absolute death rather than the death of his character. Naturally, I felt tremendously guilty about those feelings. I felt somewhat better when I learned that children of divorce often have a harder time than children who've lost a parent. Someone who has died can be sanctified and remembered with love, while it's hard to think well of a person who walks out and goes on to live another life.

From the time he left us in 1980 to the terrible moment when he was stricken, I kept hoping he'd come back and be my old dad again.

It didn't happen.
It took a deadly disease to bring us together again.
What an awful irony.

As for his affair, my own personal opinion is that Dad was caught in a situation where he believed the grass was greener. And I mean "greener" in the sense of youthful and new. Dad was so unhappy; it was almost as though he had to get out and start again.

Of course, I have my own ideas about what happened, but I wouldn't presume to say I have *the* answer. In fact, I don't think there is any one answer as to why Mom and Dad split up. Dad didn't want to be dismissed as merely the victim of a mid-life crisis. He put disclaimers out on his feelings for Mom. Later he defended his position with reporters who questioned him about his failed marriage.

"We were together for nineteen years," Dad said. "I don't consider that a failed marriage. I don't think it was a disaster. We produced some terrific kids. We just didn't grow in the same direction. We became different people. We both changed.

"To stay with someone when you no longer have anything in common is the cruelest thing to do to a child. It's much better to divorce and have two parents who are happy."

I know Dad was thinking about his own parents when he said that. Frankly, as far as he and Mother were concerned, once they separated, I didn't notice "two" happy parents for an extremely long time.

Dad suffered professionally. When the news hit the papers, the press hounded him. NBC expressed concern over his appearing in "Little House." In light of events in his own life, could he continue to enact the role of a devoted husband and father? NBC hung on. Others didn't. Dad's contract as Eastman Kodak's television spokesman was canceled.

Dad accepted every single change and alteration and went ahead. He summed up his feelings about his television image by saying, "I don't know if Charles Ingalls would have stayed married as long as he did, except that it was a long way to the next house in those days."

In the middle of the marital mess, Dad's mother, Peggy O'Neill, died. She was seventy-one years old and at the time of her death shared an apartment with Evelyn in an unfashionable part of Los

Angeles. Despite their relative proximity, Dad had seen neither his mother nor his sister in many years. In August 1981, their home was broken into, and when they filed a report, the tabloids got hold of the story. They came out with articles telling how Dad had turned his back on his mother and sister, who were living in "near poverty" while he had millions.

At the time Peggy went on record speaking about Dad, "I don't know where he lives. I never bother him because he doesn't like me asking questions. He's quite secretive. He keeps me at a distance. I don't even have his phone number. Why should I? I'm not very important. I'm just his mother."

Dad was cast as an ungrateful, ungenerous son, when in fact he had been financially helping Peggy and Evelyn for years. He provided for them, but there was still too much pain connected with those two women. No one who knew the story blamed Dad, not after the way he'd been treated. The papers, of course, never told that story; they were only concerned with presenting a dark picture.

Fuel was added to the fire of negative publicity. Dad had walked out on his wife and family. Dad shunned his mother and sister. Dad was a terrible man. The evidence piled up against him. Articles began appearing that called Dad an ego-monster. Bashing Michael Landon became a sport. I have to say, no matter what he did, Dad had the greatest heart I've ever known. It was awful to see him hurt that way.

Dad never had been a complainer; no matter how tortured his workday might have been, he kept his end up. And in the business he was in, everything was a struggle; nothing came easily. The farther he moved up the ladder of fame, the more he had to battle to maintain his position, even when he had proved himself time and again.

When he first started as Little Joe, nobody thought he was capable of producing scripts or directing. When he had shown the powers-that-be how well he could do both, you'd think they would let him do whatever he wanted. Not so. He was never accorded his just due but had to keep fighting for it. It was never "Gee, Mike, you did so great with this, we'll be happy to let you do that." Dad had to keep selling and selling himself, over and over. It's a tremendously debilitating and demanding profession, show business, and television in particular, with little thought given to the individual and his feelings.

The way the network handled the end of the run of "Bonanza" is a perfect example of the insensitive way people were treated. After being on a premier program for over ten years, the "Bonanza" cast and crew were told on a Monday that shooting would stop that Wednesday. The show had slipped in the ratings and everyone expected they would be winding down, but no one, not even original cast members like Lorne Greene and my dad, ever expected to be canceled in such a thoughtless manner. Both of them were furious at the network's treatment of the people who'd been together for all those years on a show that had for so long been a mega-hit. Dad was particularly sensitive to this kind of high-handedness. He learned a lesson from the way "Bonanza" was dumped, and he vowed he'd never allow such a thing to happen again. And he didn't.

When "Little House on the Prairie" and "Highway to Heaven" were due to end, the cast and crew were informed well in advance. They didn't have to suffer the indignity of being put out of work virtually overnight.

Dad really looked out for all the people who worked for him; they were his family, just as we at home were. It really isn't surprising that over ninety percent of the crew on "Little House" also had been with "Bonanza." And when "Highway to Heaven" went into production, the statistics stayed about the same. As someone once said of my dad, "Nobody worked *for* Mike, they worked *with* him."

Do you realize my dad never won an Emmy? Do you want to know why? In order to win, you have to nominate yourself. Dad would never do that. He'd nominate people on his shows, but never himself. My dad subscribed to the theory that "credit you give yourself is not worth having."

Dad's loyalty was impressive, especially in a business that can be positively cutthroat. He didn't pull rank or push himself into the forefront, either. He dealt with his cast and crew in a straightforward manner. With Dad you knew where you stood, and he'd never pull the rug out from under anyone. Actually, he might do it literally, but not figuratively.

Dad's pranks on the set were legendary. He so loved to laugh, he'd do anything to break people up. In NBC's televised tribute to Dad, they showed an outtake from "Little House on the Prairie" where Karen Grassle as Ma Ingalls went to the well to draw water. She dropped in the bucket and the well talked back to her! Ma

Ingalls jumped three steps back, with her mouth hanging open, as the well continued to converse. Dad had rigged the whole thing, of course, and he completely broke Karen up. He just never could resist a practical joke.

One thing he couldn't joke about, however, was his personal situation, especially once his affair was out in the open. At one point, he flew up to San Francisco to have dinner with me and to tell me his story. I was shocked at the way he looked and behaved. He seemed so defeated, so unhappy.

He had talked to Mom and told her about Cindy, the other woman. He had no idea Mom already knew from detectives she had hired to monitor his movements. From what I gather, he asked Mom to stay married to him, let him kind of sow his wild oats, have his affair, and then come back to her.

Mom wouldn't hear of it. She wouldn't be a "wimp." Dad walked out of the house in tears and said, "I'm so messed up."

He sure was.

And not only was he screwed up himself, he came close to destroying his family with remarks and behavior that were especially hurtful.

For a long while, it was just plain crushing. Mom was devastated. Dad took cheap shots.

"I never loved my wife," he told the public.

It was so ridiculous. I guess he had to go all the way around the bend to justify what he was doing. All I know is my mother was dealt blow after blow. I would never want her to be hurt like that again.

But she fought her way back. Actually, she did more than merely "come back"—she created a new life for herself out of the chaos, emerging strong and radiant.

18

What was happening to me while all this was going on? Well, I left San Francisco and moved back to Los Angeles. I liked living in the Bay City and had enjoyed much about my life there. I liked my job, and my uncle was a terrific housemate who looked out for me with loving care. I'd had a couple of boyfriends, too. But I was home-sick, and I knew it was time to go back. I returned to Los Angeles, and as events played out, it would seem to have been the right decision. In February of 1981, I met my future husband.

While I was at a Los Angeles nightclub with a friend, I saw this big, rugged, good-looking guy watching me intently. He walked over and said, "I'd like to talk." I thought he wanted to speak to someone behind me, and I stepped back.

"I don't want to get by you," he said, "I want to talk to *you*."

There was something about this man, a warmth, a naturalness, and he *was* good-looking and well-mannered. So we sat down and I talked with him. He said his name was Jim Wilson and he asked me to go out for something to eat, but I didn't want to make plans so quickly. We exchanged telephone numbers and he called me the next day. He began calling me two or three times a day for the next week or so. I finally agreed to go out with him.

Jim was from Ontario, Canada, and had come to Los Angeles to make a change in his life. He'd been a semi-pro hockey player, but at age twenty-five he'd torn a cartilage in his knee and realized he wasn't going to make it to the big time in his sport. He was looking for a new venture, when his uncle in Los Angeles invited him down to see if there might be any career potential for him in the United States.

He'd been in Los Angeles awhile and hadn't yet had much success in finding work. In fact, Jim was going back to Vancouver when we met. He decided to hang around.

Jim and I began dating. We saw each other pretty steadily for a month or so. During that whole time, I never really mentioned my family other than to talk about them in basic Mom, Dad, brother and sister terms. After we'd seen each other long enough for me to know he was interested in deepening our relationship, I told him my dad wanted to meet him. Jim was eager to meet Dad because of his feelings for me. He wanted to make a good impression on my father.

We were at my apartment when Dad arrived. I opened the door and he walked in with his girlfriend. By this time, Dad and Mom had separated and he and Cindy were openly living together. I knew she was coming and welcomed them both in.

It wasn't easy, but I had decided, right or wrong, I would stand by my dad as well as Mom. He had declared his love for someone else and made it clear she had to be accepted or he would rather not be with us.

"You want me, you must accept my decision, right or wrong," Dad had said. This was too much for some us to bear. We all tried so hard to hold on to both parents. Because it is more frightening to lose the parent who is leaving, it seemed that I tried harder to hold on to Dad. It was unbearably difficult, but none of us took sides. I could not turn my back on Dad. No matter how much I hated what had happened, I could not hate the man who had raised me. I meant no disrespect for my mother, and she knew it. Dad used me to communicate with Mom. He'd call and ask me what Mom was doing. He'd tell me what he was up to and then say, "Maybe you'll talk to your mother and tell her what I said."

I realized how confused Dad was and, believe me, I had my own share of pain and confusion. We all did. Despite her anguish, Mom never was resentful of my dealing with Dad. In her usual just manner, she reserved her hurt and anger for Dad and never let it out on me. Balance and fairness were part of Mom's character and they were the reason why she had been such a good' "base" for Dad. As much as his decision to leave tore me apart, once it was made, I had no option other than to accept my dad's choice. Otherwise, I was afraid I'd lose him. I visited with him and Cindy; I tried to be courteous and friendly. Later, after Dad married Cindy, I was glad I had not made it difficult for all of us to interact civilly.

When Dad came through the door, Jim nearly passed out, even though I had told him who my dad was. You could see his eyes pop. He told me later that he was very uncomfortable at first. I'd been concerned about his reaction, and it was one of the reasons I'd held off introducing them. I wanted to be sure Jim liked me before he knew who my dad was. I was making certain I wouldn't get into another of those Cheryl "Michael-Landon's-daughter" situations.

Dad and Jim hit it off from the beginning. Dad liked Jim because he was a real blue-collar guy, a man's man; Jim thought Dad was the same, a natural. Jim also responded to Dad's sense of humor, and he found out on their very first meeting that no one could tell a story or a joke as well as Michael Landon. Jim also couldn't get over the fact that Dad had no pretensions whatsoever and that he was so very intelligent without showing off about it.

"Your father's a genius," he told me. "I've never known anyone who read so much and had such good common sense, too. He's opinionated, for sure, but he's really sharp and funny."

Dad spoke to Jim about the special bond he and I shared. He told him about my ordeals and how proud he was of my coming through. Dad also spoke about the family unit and how important it was; he told Jim that his kids were everything to him.

"It excites me tremendously just to have my own little family where everybody loves everybody," Dad said. I remember thinking how odd it was for Dad to speak of a loving family in light of what he was doing. I realized later, that was Eugene Orowitz talking. "Ugey" was going to have a close little family unit even if he had to keep re-creating it.

★　　★　　★

159

After about six months, Jim and I got engaged. Jim had a lot of part-time jobs but still hadn't found steady employment. He desperately wanted to find a good, solid working slot.

Dad still was involved with "Little House" and another show that he'd created called "Father Murphy." Knowing that Jim was looking for employment, Dad gave him a shot at acting. Not that Jim asked, it just happened.

Jim was invited to the set one day since Dad thought that he might be perfect for a role they were trying to cast. Jim was in excellent shape and he had the perfect build for an as yet uncast role in a "Father Murphy" episode. They needed a blacksmith, and Dad figured if Jim could handle the speaking part of the role, he'd be great. He asked Jim if he was interested, and Jim said, "Sure."

Boy, I think Jim later wished he could swallow that "sure." Jim was a nervous wreck. He kept asking me if I thought he could do it, and I kept assuring him he could. To tell the truth, I had no idea if he'd be able to handle it. Remember, I'm the one who froze in front of the drama department. I know how hard it is to act, and for someone like Jim, who had no experience or even a real desire, well, who could tell?

I was at the studio with him. He was given a script with his prospective role underlined. Jim and I went off into a corner to practice reading the part. When they called Jim for the test, I gave him a smile and a hug and he was marched into Dad's office. There he read the blacksmith's lines in front of Dad and his assistants.

When the audition was over, Jim came out and sat with me. I asked him how he thought it had gone and he shrugged his shoulders.

"I have no idea, hon," he said. "I only know I felt real uncomfortable." He still seemed uncomfortable to me and shifted in his chair a lot while we waited.

Finally Dad called him back into the office. Jim managed a weak smile in my direction and went in to hear the verdict.

"How did you like it?" Dad asked.

Jim thought a bit before he answered. "Well, I have to say it's a lot more difficult than I expected."

Dad shook his head in agreement and replied, "Let me tell you something, Jim. I think one big movie star in the family is going to be enough."

Here's the whole family "hosting" the Barnum and Bailey Circus. From the left: Mike Jr., Leslie, Shawna, me, Mom, Dad holding Christopher, Nana, and Granddad. This was the day Mom confronted Dad with the information she had just learned from the detectives of his affair.

This is perhaps the last "family portrait" taken before the breakup. Dad left us right after this.

Dad and his new wife, Cindy, visiting me in a house Jim and I had rented in Sherman Oaks. I am holding my new sister, Jennifer.

My son, James Michael, nicknamed J.M., was Dad's first grandchild, and he was so very proud of him. The photo above shows Dad and my husband Jim holding J.M. In the photo on the right, Dad strolls with J.M. across the beach at Malibu.

Michael Jr., and his wife Sharee attending a birthday party for J.M. at a tiny house Jim and I had rented at Malibu Beach. After I left home I had to get used to a much more modest life style than I had grown accustomed to with Mom and Dad.

Two shots of Dad,
posing with
Shawna and me,
and mugging with
Jim and Michael
Jr.

My family always loved to party, and Halloween was a special favorite because it was also Dad's birthday. James Michael had just seen Dad's early movie *I Was a Teenage Werewolf* on television and so wanted to be just like him. Jim and I were in attendance when Dad and Cindy gave their first big Halloween party at their new Malibu Beach house.

Nana, J.M., and Aunt Woo at Eastertime. It was on the holidays that I especially missed Dad.

Dad said he left Mom because he wanted a simpler lifestyle. This is the simple little house he and Cindy built at Malibu. The landscaping followed and was truly spectacular.

One of my favorite pictures of Dad. I snapped this when he was lost in thought while looking out at the ocean. He always loved being near the water.

Note the legend on Dad's T-shirt: "I'm not deaf . . . I'm ignoring you." Michael Landon was not known for subtlety.

At the bridesmaids' luncheon given by Aunt Woo for Leslie. From the left, Leslie's close friend Kailey, me, Leslie, Sharee, and Shawna.

Dad always attended J.M.'s birthday parties and was always in charge of hanging the piñatas filled with little candies that the kids would then take turns trying to break open.

I started the tradition of taking "funny face" pictures at a Christmas gathering at Dad and Cindy's Malibu Colony beach house.

In this Christmas photo of mine, Dad is showing off his new leather jacket that Jim and I had given him.

Here's the last group shot taken of some of the Landon clan. From the left—Leslie, her husband Brian, Michael Jr. with Jennifer and Sean at his feet, Dad, Cindy, Chris, me, Shawna, and Sharee, who was seven months pregnant at the time.

The final "funny face" photo.

The Landon kids cheering on the pilot we hired to fly above the Malibu house trailing an "US" banner. Dad was in the final days of his battle with cancer and we thought this stunt might cheer him up. The pilot got so carried away, however, that he didn't seem to want to stop circling. Dad urged us to go inside so the pilot would not run out of gas and crash.

Dad loved this photo of Chris, dressed in cape and hood, playing with J.M., Sean, and Jennifer in the yard of the Malibu house. Dad loved his children and especially enjoyed hearing their laughter.

This photograph of Dad was one of his favorites and is mine as well. This is Michael Landon as I remember him. [*Charles William Bush*]

Dad's loyal fans displayed their love and concern for him during his final days by tying purple ribbons with notes attached to the fences enclosing the Malibu house.

Dad didn't live to see the birth of his first biological grandchild, but I know he is proud of our newest little angel. Ashley, daughter of Sharee and Michael, Jr., was born one month after Dad died. This picture was taken on her first birthday. [*Carousel Children's Portraiture*]

Well, Jim just started laughing and Dad joined in. Jim wasn't in the least hurt. He thought it was a great way to be told you weren't an actor.

On December 22, 1981, Jim and I slipped away and were married by a justice of the peace. I made a tape recording of the ceremony and gave it to my dad. He listened with tears in his eyes. I had dreamed of an old-fashioned church wedding, but the time wasn't right. My mom and dad were in the white heat of their divorce proceedings and my father refused to participate in the wedding ceremony if Dad was present. As a wedding present, Dad sent Jim and me to Hawaii for our honeymoon.

The early years of my marriage coincided with the breakup of my parents'. For a while, I was drawn into their conflict. I don't believe Dad and Mother spoke directly except to argue. At the outset, Dad asked me to let him know what my mother was doing and how she was reacting. Of course, I was very guarded about telling him anything about Mother. I don't think any of us wanted him to know how utterly devastated she was. At that point I feel he still hoped to effect a reconciliation. Later, when they'd officially parted, most of his queries had to do with the kids and were as simple as Dad's wanting me to ask if Shawna and Chris could join him and Cindy for a weekend, or something of that nature.

I didn't like being a go-between; it was a very difficult situation. For a time it even threatened to dampen my own newfound happiness, and certainly the joy of creating my own new home was tempered by watching the disintegration of the one that I had known and cherished for so long.

In many ways the structure of the Landon family already had started to crumble, or at least change.

Because I was nine years older than my nearest sibling and twenty-one years older than the youngest, I was able to see things differently and understand parts of the divorce. Still, we were all very confused and hurt.

It was very hard at the beginning because Dad was so conflicted about what he was doing. He couldn't help himself, and yet he didn't want to lose Mom and his family. He wanted her to hang in and allow him to work through things. He thought the grass was greener because so many things in his life had become gray.

Yes, he and Mom had drifted apart; they were on different wave-lengths even for something as simple as his having to go to bed early and Mom's being a night person. And, of course, they were getting older. Dad couldn't afford to look old because of his work. Consequently he had plastic surgery on his face. Dad was quite open about what he did and informed the press himself. He did this with humor, making those around him feel as comfortable as he was.

The celebrity life gnawed at him, too. As I said, he'd created this palace for us, given us everything, and then he resented the change and wanted a return to the simpler life. This time, however, the "simpler" life he craved seemed to include having a wife and a family and a mistress. He was desperate to hold on to his family and, given time, he believed he could work things out. Mom could not accept such an arrangement. Fish or cut bait; sink or swim— these were her convictions. She would not be intimidated by Dad. I think she was exhibiting the exact kind of moxie Dad had always wanted to see in her. Unfortunately, this show of back-bone and independence worked against their union rather than for it.

Dad enjoyed money and power, but he didn't like the trappings that went with it. He'd conditioned the entire family to like and expect some of those trappings, but of all of us, Mom was the one most trapped by it.

Through witnessing my parents' divorce, I would conclude that the woman is really put through the wringer if the man is the only breadwinner in the relationship. Everything my mother had done to build Dad up and to help him achieve his goals was ignored. She was shown little or no respect and was made to feel like an outsider, a beggar, rather than the equal partner she had been. She was dealt with in a condescending and patronizing manner. It was very cruel and very wrong.

And somewhere deep in his heart, Dad had to know just how unfair all this was. He couldn't admit it, however. He had to build a wall and create a distance between all of us and him so that he didn't have to deal with the bitter truth of the situation. He did this not only with us but with most of the friends he and Mom shared. I don't think he could handle their obvious shock and dismay at the way he was behaving. So, for a while anyway, he turned his back on them as well. It was as though he'd taken an ax and hacked his life into two pieces: that which came before the breakup, and that which came after. It took a long time for the family to bridge the gap. Sadly, it was his impending death that forged the last link that finally reunited us.

_19_

*M*om and Dad were divorced in December 1981, the same month I was married. A year and a half later they were still fighting over the community property settlement. I know my dad was surprised at Mom's tenacity. She refused to lie down and let anyone walk over her, especially someone who'd been walking beside her for so many years.

I was sickened when someone told me that one of the tabloids actually had printed a list of Mom's estimated monthly living expenses. Putting something that was so emotional into dollars and cents made matters even worse. And I'm sure the amounts seemed extravagant to many who have not had the experience of a celebrity life-style, but what does any of it truly matter? Who bothers to think that the woman may be going through emotional agony on which no dollar value could be placed?

When it was finally over, my mom emerged from the divorce financially secure and emotionally ravaged. As I said, though, she didn't stay down for long. With a number of other wives of celebrities whose spouses had walked out on them, she helped to form an organization called LADIES. LADIES, an acronym for "Life After Divorce Is Eventually Sane," was founded in 1983, and among the charter members were the ex-wives of Ken Berry, Gene Hackman,

165

George Segal, Jerry Lewis, Gavin MacLeod, Don Knotts, Leonard Nimoy, and Glen Campbell.

In the beginning, LADIES provided an opportunity for these suddenly abandoned women to get together and deal with the painful experience of a Hollywood fishbowl divorce. The first meeting was mind-blowing for all of them. Mom and a few others were in the midst of their divorces and finding no sympathy (certainly not in the press) because they were getting big money settlements. Money, however, can't erase the pain and trauma of a breakup and divorce. And all the money in the world doesn't make up for the indignity of having a man who once adored you call your marriage a "mistake" on TV. Nor does it make up for having to deal with children whose lives are shattered. Mom may have received a hefty settlement—hey, this is Hollywood, after all—but it did nothing to erase the emotional battering she suffered or to erase the memory of public humiliation. Divorce in Hollywood is the same as divorce anywhere, only played out on a big screen and in living color.

LADIES has grown in importance and influence over the years. Mom has gone around the country to speak in front of large audiences and even has appeared on television to spread the word. Mom, who used to tremble at the thought of going on camera, became a real spokesperson for women's rights. She believed so fervently in the cause, it forced her to overcome her shyness and her fear of speaking in public. And it's a good thing, too. LADIES actually has helped to enact legislation benefiting women.

And not only did my mother get involved in a political cause, she also blossomed into a sharp businesswoman. She opened a boutique in Beverly Hills called Trio. Ironically, my dad used Mom's success after the breakup to help absolve himself of some of his guilt.

"I think Lynn is a much happier person now than she was when we were married," Dad said about the post-divorce Mom. "She's a much more energetic person and I can see the change in her. She's her own person. She has her own business, something I wish she would have done years ago, but she never did. I think the divorce really brought her out, made her a more rounded person than she was before. At least I would like to think so because she's a good person."

Today, Mom has made a whole new life for herself. She took the miserable hand she was dealt and turned it into a grand slam. She has shown the world what kind of moxie she's made of. And she hasn't lacked for male companionship, either. She dates, but hasn't wanted to make a commitment—not yet at least. She has lots of stories about some of the awkwardness of those early days of dating. One in particular made me laugh because it was so typical of Mom. She was out with a gentleman and when he brought her home she invited him in for a few minutes.

"Would you like something to drink?" asked Mom.

"A cup of coffee would be great," he answered.

Mom laughed. "You know," she told him, "I could get you any kind of soft drink or wine or mix you a cocktail, but I don't know how to make coffee."

Good old Mom. And I bet she still doesn't know how to make coffee.

Today we can laugh at some of the problems we all had in adjusting to life without Dad, but for a long time, the funny moments really were few and far between. It was hard on all of us, but it was worst for Mom. She had to be there for us, and tending to the family's wounds was her toughest job.

At first, the little ones clung to her in hurt and confusion. Mom could have seized an opportunity in those early months to turn them against Dad forever, but she just isn't that kind of person. She wanted them to work their way through their grief, to accept the divorce, accept Dad's remarriage, and find some kind of happiness on their own. Mom found solace in God. She became a born-again Christian, and so did Leslie and Michael, Jr.

When the divorce became final, when Dad pulled away from us, I suffered from a profound feeling of loss, a feeling so intense that I nearly lost myself in my personal despair. I hadn't realized how dependent I was on my dad's love. His leaving raised all the old abandonment issues again. I simply couldn't handle losing him because he was the one person I couldn't lose. Difficulties began to escalate.

First I'd lost my dad, or at least the dad I knew and loved; and then I lost my health. I reinjured my knee and had to have surgery. Also, I felt I'd lost my looks; my beautiful long hair was butchered in a beauty parlor and I had to cut it all off to try and salvage my appearance. And to top it off, we didn't have the money to pay for all these things.

I don't want to imply that I was suddenly cut off by my dad. He had always been generous, and still gave me a monthly stipend, but it just wasn't enough to keep Jim and me going, not with my mounting medical bills. My husband was doing his utmost to establish a career. He answered ads, pounded the pavements and did everything he could to get himself started. Until that happened, however, we still had to eat, and so he took a job as a waiter. I was so busy going back and forth from home to hospital that I couldn't hold down a steady job. It was awfully tough for a while.

Because he wasn't college-educated, the only viable option for Jim seemed to be in independent sales. He started out with a solar-energy firm and I helped him with phone solicitations. Remember, I was the girl from CEDU who wowed them over the phone. I worked out of the house and sometimes we did okay, at least on paper. I learned how difficult it can be to collect the money you've earned. One company owed us fifteen thousand dollars, but before we were paid, the company went bankrupt. Another time we worked for a reputable man in the leather business. Lo and behold, that reputable man sent us checks twice and they bounced both times.

For eight long years, Jim and I struggled. Many times we were desperate for enough money to get by, but out of this desperation came maturity.

I began to devise ways to raise money. I even arranged to trade off work for medical help, such as doing office work for a doctor. Then, when there wasn't any more work for me to do, I went without treatment.

When I became pregnant, Jim and I were both elated. Maybe we couldn't afford a child, but it was something we had prayed for, and somehow, we'd manage.

James Michael arrived on September 22, 1984. Dad said, "He'll be as tough as his mother and with my good looks."

Cindy, Dad's new wife, had given birth to their first child, Jennifer, a year before my son, Dad's first grandson, was born.

After James was born, I went through a terrible period. I felt rejected and needy. Part of my problem, of course, may have been post-partum depression, but I also had a ruptured disc. I gained fifty pounds during my pregnancy and didn't lose the last twenty-five all that quickly. I looked awful.

Dad noticed. Jim told me Dad pulled him aside one day and asked, "What's the matter with Cheryl? Why has she let herself go like this?"

The man who once seemed to read my every thought couldn't figure out what had happened.

Jim and I and little James Michael struggled on. We lived in a series of houses, some of them very small, but all of which had yards—I couldn't bear the thought of not having a yard for our son.

We rented a house in Camarillo. I really liked it there; it reminded me of Encino in the old days. And, at last, good things started to happen. Jim went into business with a close acquaintance and became a vice president and partner in a very successful salvage company, Damielle Metal. The days of financial desperation were drawing to a close.

I got myself back into shape again physically. My hair grew long, I slimmed down, and the sparkle came back into my eyes. Dad saw the change and was obviously very pleased. I saw the love and admiration in his eyes and I heard him say proudly, "You got it back, baby, you got it back!" Suddenly, I realized Dad might have had his own purpose in standing back, in distancing himself. Because he wasn't there to bail me out, for the first time I truly had to rely on myself. Finally I had been weaned away from clinging, childish needs.

And yes, I *did* get it back. I *did* pull myself up. I became the daughter, the strong and independent woman Dad had always wanted me to be. In a very special way, I had Dad to thank for this growth, and for my new independence. I learned to use my own resources rather than continually run to him or Mom. At last I was standing on my own two feet.

What I did not know at the time, of course—what none of us knew—was that just as I started living again, Dad was dying.

20

*I*n March of 1991, Dad and his new family went on a skiing holiday to Park City, Utah. They were all thrilled to be getting away, no one more than Dad. He'd finished doing the pilot for "Us" and wanted to take a vacation before starting production in June. Everyone was in good spirits, or seemed to be. No one, not even his wife, knew that Dad's lighthearted behavior was a cover-up. He was not feeling well and, in fact, had become quite concerned about his health.

It started out innocently enough. Around Christmas, Dad found that his appetite had greatly diminished. Cindy had been concerned about his eating habits for some time, and had been after him to make some changes. She herself favored health foods and couldn't stand to watch Dad pack away such a careless and unbalanced diet. She told their doctor about her husband's poor nutritional practices and he advised Dad to mend his ways or suffer the consequences. Dad merely laughed it off and turned the whole thing into a joke.

"I eat like a horse," he said, "and horses get along fine."

It wasn't just the way he ate, or even what he ate. He had a number of unhealthy habits. For example, Dad smoked a lot. My husband Jim told me Dad positively loved smoking, almost as much as he loved drinking. Jim's theory is, if you drink, you smoke, and Dad was a perfect example of this premise. Dad preferred Carltons and treated each cigarette as if it were his last, drawing the smoke in "all the way down to his toes." He'd toss down vodka with the same abandonment. Jim said Dad preferred cheap, rotgut stuff rather than expensive brands. He drank it straight, too, without any ice cubes or mixer.

Jim spent a fair amount of time with my dad and that time usually involved talking and drinking. Dad spoke freely with Jim on a man-to-man basis, and, of course, Jim was just about the only person in the family who'd join Dad in drinking. Mom rarely drank, and we followed her lead.

According to Jim, Dad put most of the blame for leaving us on his dissatisfaction with the Beverly Hills scene and his vulnerability to a younger woman. I always felt that he might have been able to deal with the former if the latter hadn't come along, and what Jim learned from Dad served to corroborate my assessment. Also, Dad wasn't good at confrontation and he hated conflict of any kind. Jim pointed out that his track record proved he would opt to take the easier way out, rather than to deal with contention. Sometimes that meant relying on people who could step in and do the hard dealing or dirty work for him. That's why he had people like his longtime associate, Kent McCray, working with him.

Jim was right, and I learned something from watching my dad in these situations: Problems are never solved by walking away from them, and you have to deal with them yourself. Eventually, if you work at it, things will be resolved. They might not be settled in the manner you expected, and you may not get everything you want, but still, you've got to hang in there and see it through. Dad didn't. He ran and then had to find reasons to justify what he did. "Your dad was a writer," Jim said to me, "and like any good storyteller, he could rewrite his own story." Jim was right again.

Dad told Jim about all the deals he was making and the enormous amount of money he was pulling in: "You know, Jim honey, I'm really good at making money, but I'm terrible at managing it."

Dad was "the big player and had the responsibility of making the money," yet he couldn't make decisions about his personal management. Once again, he chose to listen to others. Jim said Dad left it to his new wife to dictate the direction of the funds that had been set up for us kids—which made it very awkward for us.

Jim remembered one time when Dad was going to check on some

deal with him in Arizona, with the possibility of assisting him in the investment. Dad's words were, "Make this work quick, because if I'm going to do it, I have to do it fast 'cause I'm getting opposition at home."

Jim heard and saw a lot, some of which wasn't always pleasant, yet through it all, he retained enormous respect and regard for Dad.

"I felt very inferior coming from a simple background and moving into such a wealthy arena," my husband confessed, "but of all the people in your family, Mike was the one who made me feel most comfortable. And if anyone had the right to feel bigger and better, it sure was your dad."

Dad and Jim's male bonding made them especially close, like old school buddies. Sometimes, they'd sit out at Dad's new house in Malibu and Dad would talk on and on. Jim was a good audience and always respectful of Dad's confidences. He never revealed any of the things Dad told him until after Dad was gone, and even now I suspect he knows things he hasn't told me.

One thing Jim did reveal was that as much as he enjoyed being with Dad, he always was concerned with his excessive smoking. Unfortunately, as is so often the case in such situations, he didn't feel he was the person to say anything about it, and so he kept his mouth shut. We knew, of course, that Dad wanted to stop; he just couldn't. He did ease off a bit when his dear friend and colleague Victor French died of lung cancer in May of 1989. Victor, like Dad, was a heavy smoker and his death rocked Dad.

Victor's roles in "Little House" and "Highway to Heaven" paralleled Dan Blocker's Hoss in "Bonanza." Like Dan, Victor was a big guy, but the resemblance ended there. Dan was "the gentle giant" and the character Hoss had been an extension of that image. Victor's career had been built on his portrayals of villains. He could project meanness like nobody else and spent twenty years on both the big and little screens appearing invariably as a killer or a rapist. Dad saw something unique behind his menacing demeanor and cast him as a good guy, for which Victor was eternally grateful. They became good pals, and after Victor's death Dad did try to cut back on cigarettes. He never stopped drinking, though. His consumption of alcohol—particularly vodka—was monumental. Excessive drinking, excessive smoking, and poor eating habits—all were negative factors in Dad's health.

*   *   *

Dad's normally large appetite began to diminish. At first, he experienced abdominal pains and an unaccustomed feeling of fullness in his stomach. He didn't mention it to anyone at the time, however. He thought it might be an ulcer. Seven months passed with him suffering constant distress and hiding it from everyone.

In March, when the pain became unbearable, he finally decided to see someone. Without informing the family, he went to see a doctor before the Utah ski trip. He had an upper GI series done and was relieved when the doctors found nothing wrong except for an unusual amount of acidity. The doctor recommended antacid pills and told Dad the cramps could easily be stress-related. Dad rejected the "stress" theory; he said he never felt stress in his work because he liked what he did so much.

He began taking the antacid pills and went to Utah, still without telling anyone he'd seen the doctor. Once there, things didn't improve; they got worse. Suddenly, he experienced piercing stomach cramps, pain so severe that he doubled over in agony. Finally he was forced to acknowledge that something was definitely wrong, though he never suspected it was anything life-threatening. He flew back to Los Angeles and went to the hospital for further tests. Cindy and the kids stayed in Utah.

The doctor examined Dad and ordered a CAT scan. Nothing was said, but Dad was suspicious when the doctor told him he would check the results and call him at ten-thirty in the evening. As Dad put it, "Doctors tend not to work until ten-thirty unless something is cocky-doo-doo." If this doctor was going to get in touch with him so promptly, something *really* must be wrong.

Dad spent a nervous day. The first thing the doctor said when he called that evening was for Dad to get his wife back home.

"What have I got?" Dad asked. The doctor told him there was a large tumor in his abdomen and they would do a biopsy the next day. A tumor? A biopsy? Poor Dad had to hear those first ominous words about his condition when he was alone.

Dad was admitted to Cedars-Sinai Medical Center on April 3, 1991. He was taken to room 8215, an elegantly furnished private suite with a huge bay window, offering a panoramic view that included the famous "Hollywood" sign. Dad could sit in his room and see the large white letters looming over the city. I don't think the scenery provided much solace, however.

The doctor couldn't believe Dad had waited so long to come in for tests. He couldn't imagine how anyone could go through such terrible pain without seeking relief. Ironically, according to one tabloid, the doctor was supposed to have said that had Dad "not adhered to a perfect diet and exercise his entire life, he likely would be dead already." That statement gives you a good idea either of how inaccurate reporting can be, or how fooled doctors can be.

A liver biopsy was ordered, and after the procedure the specimen was rushed through the pathology lab.

Dad did not want to hear the results of the biopsy while in the hospital, however; he wanted to be at home. He had the doctor discharge him from Cedars. So on the next day, on April 5, at his Malibu ranch with his wife at his side, Dad was told the awful news. He had adenocarcinoma, cancer of the pancreas, about as bad a cancer as anyone can get. Dad even made a joke out of that, asking why they gave "the longest names to the diseases that give you the shortest time to live." Throughout his illness, Dad made many jokes trying to lighten the burden for us, and, I'm sure, for himself. I think Dad felt he could handle anything he could make light of, even death.

These were the facts: there were two spots on his liver, one approximately an inch across, the other around half an inch. The cancer already was inoperable.

The news "shocked the hell" out of Dad. He couldn't believe it. He told the doctor he'd only been in a hospital once before. He asked if there might be some mistake, perhaps a misdiagnosis, maybe he should be retested. The doctor shook his head, no. There was no mistake. Dad struggled to keep from losing his composure. He didn't want to fall apart in front of his wife.

He had been given a death sentence. He was only fifty-four years old; except for the battle with encephalitis, he had been healthy all his life. He was a good athlete and had kept himself in shape with hard workouts. He could bench-press up to three hundred and fifty pounds. None of that mattered now. Despite his workouts and strengthening exercises, he'd misused his body and he knew it.

Heavy drinking, smoking, and a poor diet had wreaked havoc on his system. If you do those kinds of things to your body, "even if you think you're too strong to get anything," Dad wrote, "somehow you're going to pay." And other things started to go wrong as well. Earlier we had noticed signs of depression, something very uncommon for Dad. Now they were very much a part of his existence.

What do you do when you're told you're going to die? We all have to face death someday—that's a given. And in truth, we may have faced it many times and not even known. Dad had.

In 1988 there was a macabre incident involving a mental patient who was wanted in connection with several homicides in New Mexico. He had come to Hollywood in December and gone on the tour at Universal Studios. While traveling around the lot, he told some people he was on a "mission from God," and asked employees where he could find Michael Landon. The people at Universal had no idea where Dad was because he never had done anything at that studio. At the time, Dad was working at MGM, which was in Culver City, nearly twenty miles away from Universal. He was filming an episode of "Highway to Heaven," and totally unaware that a maniac was stalking him.

Since no one seemed to know where Michael Landon was, the man got off the sightseeing-tour bus and went back to the entrance gate. He walked up to the guardhouse and said he had to use a studio phone to speak to Michael Landon. The guards wouldn't allow it, and he stormed off.

A few minutes later he reappeared, pulled out a gun and shot both guards. One of them was killed instantly; the other died later in the hospital. Those poor souls had to pay the price because a crazed man got it into his head that Dad was at Universal Studios. Naturally when Dad heard the news, he was shaken, but he had to slough it off and go on.

Now he was being stalked by a killer infinitely more frightening than a deranged mental patient. This time no one else would take the bullets meant for him. His celebrity had not caused this terrifying thing, and his celebrity could not save him. This time he could not shrug it off and go on.

Dad said he never had time to stand on a hilltop and scream, but then he wasn't the kind to rail against his fate. As he wrote in *Life* magazine, "There's a kind of person who, when he gets a jolt like this, says, 'Well, I'm gonna die, and that's the end of it.' They just put on the pajamas and waste away. But," Dad added in a true indication of his character, "that's not fair. Not fair to yourself, not fair to your family, not fair to people you don't even know. Because if you fight and win, it pays off for thousands of people. It gives them hope, and hope can work miracles."

This attitude was typical of my dad, this way of rising to the occasion as nobly as any of the characters he'd ever portrayed. It was not an attitude he followed consistently, however. From the beginning, his television scripts had given people faith while gently guiding them toward a certain kind of positive thinking. "I made people reach into their lives and look for a higher power, God or even themselves, to solve their problems." Parents wrote letters telling Dad they raised their own children following the example set by the Ingallses. Dad was pleased by such praise but didn't consider it a personal endorsement. He was emphatic about his character not taking credit for the solutions. He'd always drawn a clear distinction between the fictional persons he portrayed and Michael Landon the man. His fans might confuse the personalities; he didn't.

When he and Mom got divorced and he was told he was committing professional suicide because he wasn't acting like Charles Ingalls, Dad had quickly stated, "I'm not Charles Ingalls!"

This time there was a merging between his television personalities and his real self; it was something he'd never done before, consciously or unconsciously. Now, in the hour of his death, he was ready and willing to act like the heroes he'd created. Why? Perhaps because it wasn't "fair." He couldn't give up because he was aware of all the people who looked to him for guidance. Before, he had written scripts about life experiences that served as examples for people, and these scripts conveyed messages he wanted people to believe and follow, whether or not he necessarily followed them himself. Well, this time he couldn't write a script. This time, if he wanted to provide an example for others to follow, he would have to live it. This time, *Michael Landon* would have to be the example.

21

*T*he day after Dad told us about the cancer, Jim and I drove over to his house in Malibu. Dad had called all of his children and requested us to gather together with him. We sat in the family room and Dad spoke very quietly and matter-of-factly about what had happened. I had spent the previous day and evening crying my eyes out. I hadn't slept. I could see that my brothers and sisters had had the same experience. We were all red-eyed and filled with pain and fear. The expression on Dad's face was so very, very sad. I really can't remember his exact words, I think he said something about his planning to put up a good fight and wanting us to help him. He also repeated exactly what the doctors had told him.

Stunned silence followed his statement. When you hear the kind of news we were hearing, you can't absorb it immediately; it takes time for it to sink in.

After he'd said his piece, Dad stood there looking at all of us. Then the weeping began, punctuated by cries of "oh, no" and "oh, God." It was an experience I would hope never to relive. And through it all Dad stood there looking at us with love and sadness. We all got up and went to him, each hugging him in turn and crying in his arms.

Dad allowed us to grieve with him for a while, and then he called a halt. He told us he wanted us to get the tears out of our systems, and from that day on, we were to get behind him in a positive way. He needed our support. He asked us for our love without tears, and from then on, that's what we tried to give him.

"I'm not the kind of a person who gives up without a fight," Dad wrote in his revealing essay in *Life* magazine.

If I'm gonna die, Death's gonna have to do a lot of fighting to get me. I'm not just gonna lie down and let it happen. I've got too much I don't want to leave. Mainly my family. I'm in the fight of my life but I don't know if I'd be fighting if I didn't have my family. The doctors would say, We can't really do anything for you, you're going to die. And I would say, O.K., I've had a good life. Enough happiness, enough success. Now I won't have to worry about the new series making it or not. And that would be that, if it was just me. But it *isn't* just me.

I love my work too [continued Dad]. I've had three successful series, and I want to find out if I can make a fourth. And I'm that close to doing it. The pilot for "Us" is ready to air, and it's a good pilot. Yesterday I called Jeff Sagansky, the entertainment chief at CBS, and I told him, "Jeff, this is the worst goddamn deal you've made since you bought baseball." And he was great. I told him I had to stop work on the series until I got better and he said he wouldn't air the pilot till I had the next twelve episodes ready. Gives me one more thing to shoot for.

And I'm shooting. I'm going to beat this cancer or die trying.

When he wrote the article for *Life,* Dad already had learned his condition had worsened; he was going to die. The cancer had spread into an area near his kidneys; the tumor on his pancreas was the size of a softball and was pressing against his stomach. Dad's response? "I can't pretend I've got a hangnail."

Immediately after the family was apprised of the situation, Dad felt he had to protect his children, especially the little ones. Three days after he was told he had cancer, he had his publicist call a press conference; he wanted to address the media himself. Dad thought that by coming forward and telling the truth, he could forestall the ugly stories which were bound to start circulating.

Dad was forthright always. Way back when I'd had my problems, he wouldn't let me hide. He'd made me come forward and speak through the press to all the kids who might be having the same problems. I remember being rather fearful and hesitant about going public, but Dad said it had to be done to help educate others. So I discussed my problem in a candid and revealing magazine article, which some tabloids then took and twisted out of proportion. That's what I got for being straightforward. It was very hurtful.

On the day of the press conference, reporters and photographers gathered at Dad's house and set up the cameras and other equipment in the backyard. At the time, no one knew what they were going to hear. Certainly the rumor of Dad's illness had been circulating, but what the illness was and the full extent of it hadn't yet been revealed. Most of the members of the press liked Dad. He'd always been willing to share his story with the public.

I watched that conference and was filled with admiration for my dad. He was magnificent.

He wore a green shirt and khaki pants and looked tanned and trim as he walked onto the patio and sat down on a wrought-iron chair. He began the conference with a joke.

"Boy, you gotta be real sick to get this much attention," he laughed when he caught sight of the hordes of newsmen and cameramen.

Over the next thirty minutes, Dad did his best to appear casual and controlled. He couldn't help cracking jokes even after he'd told the press what the nature of his disease was.

"I want my agent to know that this shoots to hell any chance of my doing a health-food commercial," Dad said sarcastically. The reporters were stunned and grabbed on to any of Dad's quips that might relieve them of the awful tension. Many of them simply couldn't believe what they were hearing, that they were interviewing a dying man; especially since the dying man was the incredibly lively Michael Landon.

Dad tried so gamely to keep positive emotions up. He said that his role in "Highway to Heaven" might have helped him because "I played a dead guy." Dad's attempts at levity went right by most of the members of the press. It's awfully hard to laugh when a man is telling you he's going to die. Dad persisted and then, seeing the looks on the faces of his audience, said he had to treat this in the way he did because he had "a sense of humor about everything." Even as he said the words, you could see he was struggling. He swallowed a couple of times and then started to explain his illness.

He told the reporters he really didn't find much to laugh about in his situation, but if he was going to beat it, he had to come out and fight and not cower in a corner.

"I think all of us create our own miracles," Dad declared.

He went on to say that at first he didn't believe the news the doctors had given him. Aside from his stomach pains, he felt fine. And since he always had been a physically fit person, he found it hard to accept that he could feel so well yet be so sick. He claimed that right after he heard the news, he began doing push-ups "just to make sure I was just as strong as I was the day before." He continued doing the push-ups every day for a while, saying that he figured if he could do that, he could beat the cancer.

A few of the reporters asked Dad to do a few push-ups for them on the patio. Unable to resist a challenge and eager to show he still was fit, Dad got out of his chair and did a few exercises.

As I watched him I felt such a mixture of pain and pride. He was so game, so anxious to keep things going as they had been, and I loved and admired him for that. What worried him, Dad told the reporters, was what was happening to the people working on his new series.

"It's kind of a dirty trick to do to your co-stars when they finally get a break and the series sells." Dad added there was no way he could continue with the show as long as this thing was hanging over him.

He mentioned he was going to have chemotherapy and talked to the press about his weight. He told them he felt terrific except for the trouble he had digesting food. He admitted he had lost weight and was down about six pounds from his ideal of 160.

"I've become a papaya-juice lover," he explained. Dad waxed eloquent over papaya because he'd learned it helps the digestive system.

I remember it was a beautiful sunny day and the shadows played across Dad's face as he sat there talking. I could see the tension around his lips and the sorrow in his eyes and the defiant way he held his chin, and still he talked on calmly. I think it was one of his greatest performances.

At the conclusion, Dad said very simply, "Life has been good to me. It's not like I missed an awful lot. I had a pretty good lick here. I am going to fight it. Every moment gets a little more important after something like this." Then he paused and looked straight at the camera. "So, live every minute, guys."

Dad stood up and walked across the patio and into the house. When he reached the door, he turned for a moment, raised his fist, and disappeared.

The interview was over.

The circus began.

22

*T*hat evening the network newscasts broadcast the story. NBC gave it extra coverage because even though Dad had gone to CBS with his new project, he'd been an NBC mainstay for nearly thirty years. CNN's "Headline News" broadcast the story all evening, and the news was heard around the world.

The next morning, there wasn't a newspaper in the country that didn't run the story of Dad's illness, and most of them put it on the front pages. Millions of fans who loved him were despondent, and even those who hadn't been hard-core supporters expressed their sorrow and their admiration for Dad's courage. Dad had touched the heartstrings of the public again, only this time it wasn't through a fictionalized story based on real-life experiences. This time it was the experience itself.

Once the world had been informed, Dad dug in and began his battle. He consulted with top experts and specialists in the field of oncology. They recommended chemotherapy in high doses, standard medical procedure for pancreatic cancer.

"That's the only hope they see," wrote Dad. But he also knew that chemotherapy's rate of success was "really zero. Less than one percent of the patients treated are alive at the end of five years. And," continued Dad, "I'm not sure in these cases what alive

185

means." Dad was well aware of the horrendous effects that huge doses of chemotherapy had on the body: the sores in the mouth, the peeling skin, the hair falling out and the gradual breakdown of major organs. "It's bad enough I have white roots," Dad joked, "let alone no roots!"

"You can die of the cure before you die of the disease," he commented. Despite his feelings, however, he wanted others to know he wasn't knocking chemotherapy in general. "There are many types of cancer, and for some of them chemotherapy's success rate is spectacular," he wrote, continuing, "I'm just saying that for the kind of cancer I've got, the evidence says it's useless."

Notwithstanding Dad's doubts and because the doctors recommended it, he decided to undergo the procedure. A few days after the press conference, he had his first treatment.

Dad had almost stopped eating because he got such terrible abdominal cramps after he ate. Consequently, he was experiencing rapid weight loss. To counteract this decline, the doctors suggested he drink a mixture of raw eggs and milk. He'd throw the ingredients into a blender and take the stuff several times a day. The problem was, every time he drank the eggs and milk, his cramps would get worse. Now, stronger painkillers were prescribed.

"Soon," wrote Dad, "I was in a terrible cycle: fattening drink, unbearable pain, painkiller, wacky state of mind, and then at night I'd take a sleeping pill. Day after day the same pattern. Believe me, pain pills drag your ass down. They give you a bit of a buzz, so it's easy to fall into the trap, and before you know it, there's no fight left in you. You're wandering around like a zombie in pajamas. You're history."

The dilemma Dad faced happens to many cancer patients. They have to make a choice for a living death which may lead to life or may not. As Dad himself said, "I could go through all this, and at the end of the road there was a ninety-nine percent guarantee that I'd be dead. Now I don't mind dying if I have to, but I'm damned if I want to pay for the guarantee. I'm sorry."

Despite his misgivings, Dad tried the chemo. He got a single shot, a small dose of 5-FU, which he said was a "basic type of chemotherapy—sort of like testing the water with my toe." He knew that later the doctors would add the ingredients that tear up the body and just the thought of it made him ill.

"I had an adverse reaction even before the treatment," he wrote. "Right before the injection I took a tennis lesson, and on the court I felt as weak as a baby. Not because I was sick. I felt weak because I was thinking about the goddamn chemo going into me."

Dad loathed the treatment. "I hated the thought of being injected with deadly chemicals and having no control over my life. So I decided to stop chemotherapy, at least for now, and try something different."

The something different was a holistic program of diet and exercise. One of the oncologists Dad consulted specialized in using a treatment that combined traditional and nontraditional methods. Dad was told this doctor had been a consultant when President Ronald Reagan had his colon-cancer treatments.

The doctor's program called for eating healthy foods and supplementing the diet with vitamins. The patient was urged to get as much exercise as possible and encouraged to use stress-management techniques including hypnosis.

Dad embraced the program and turned overnight from Mr. Meat-and-Potatoes to Mr. Organic. At least a dozen times a day he would consume a twelve-ounce glass of organic juice blended of apples, carrots, and beet tops. Not only that, typical of Dad, he had to become his own authority on nutrition. He read any and every book he could get his hands on and would expound in detail to all of us.

"It's the pectin in apples that helps digestion," he said. "And the vegetables I eat are all high in enzymes to replace the digestive juices my pancreas has stopped producing. The carotene in carrots is supposed to kill cancer cells, but," Dad joked, "those damn carrots are turning me orange."

Dad adhered to a strict organic diet consisting of raw vegetables, beans and lentils three times a day. He also took coffee enemas. Everything was carried out under the doctor's supervision. Dad was thrilled when the stomach pains lessened after a few days and he found himself able to eat again, albeit lightly. He gained some weight, and continued to play tennis and work out.

The upsurge was brief; he could tell he was getting weaker. He decided to conserve his strength and cut down on physical exertion. He no longer did morning push-ups or played an afternoon tennis game.

Despite the setback, Dad chose to stick with the program. He said he would continue it for a month and a half, and see what happened. Then, if the cancer hadn't stopped growing, he would reassess the situation.

Meanwhile, the diet seemed to be strengthening his immune system. He was taking hormones to build up his red-cell count. Once his resistance improved, the doctors could try experimental procedures.

All during his illness, Dad was besieged with letters and telephone calls. They came from the rich and famous and the poor and unknown. Nancy Reagan telephoned and couldn't help crying. Dad tried to make *her* feel better and said, "Nancy, come on, now. It's going to be all right."

Another old friend called and said, "You sound great, Mike."

"Why shouldn't I?" Dad answered. "It's not my voice that's sick."

Not only was Dad struggling to overcome his disease, he was battling to keep up everyone's spirits, especially that of the little ones. My heart went out to his two youngest children, Jennifer and Sean. Dad spent much time with them trying to make them feel better and to reassure them that even if he had to leave them, they'd never be alone.

This was the Michael Landon who had rescued and reassured a frightened little girl some thirty years before. This same man was now assuring his children they would always be safe. Only this time he wouldn't be around to make it okay himself.

Dad said it was more painful for him to deal with the children's fears than his own agony. He knew he had to appear brave and confident before them. Children are so quick to catch the slightest hint of something wrong. They're like little lie detectors and you can't fool them if you don't act convincingly.

Again, Dad gave brilliant performances. He'd sit with the kids and joke and laugh, and then he'd seriously address the future. He'd never lost his touch with children. He knew just how to talk to them.

Practically the first thing he told Jennifer and Sean was that they couldn't "catch" what he had. See, Dad had this real sense of what kids worry about. By immediately allaying their natural fears for their own health, he could then tell them about his condition.

He knew they would miss him terribly and he wished more than anything he didn't have to go, but, if he did, everything would be just as it had been; they would be safe in the hands of their mother. He told them that though he might have to go away, their mother would be there and she was young and strong. And they had all their brothers and sisters ready and willing to help.

We were, too.

A couple of weeks after Dad started his organic regime, he rejected the doctor whose plan he'd been following. The doctor began showing up on television and radio talking about his treatment for his patients and using Dad's name, almost as though it were an endorsement. He'd never asked Dad's permission, and further investigation showed the doctor might not have been as involved in Ronald Reagan's cancer treatment as Dad was led to believe. It goes to show you that even someone as protected and privileged as my dad was an open target.

On April 24, Dad went to the hospital for a second CAT scan. He'd actually been feeling better and thought he'd get some good news. What he heard devastated him. The tumor had doubled in size and the cancer had spread to his colon.

23

MICHAEL LANDON: IT'S OVER.

Such was the tabloid headline displayed in supermarkets all across America in late April of 1991. Despite all Dad's efforts to snuff the sensationalist press, they weren't about to let the story of his fatal illness slide by. Never mind the fact that Dad was fighting to live, that he still hadn't given up; the story of his impending death was too hot, too big, so they gave up for him. My dad saw that headline, and so did the rest of the family. You can guess how it affected us.

I hope that people who read the tabloids understand that hearsay and exaggeration are the mainstays of their reporting. I saw examples of it many times; from the reports of my own brush with drugs to the many episodes of my dad's life which were covered in the most scandalous and overstated ways possible.

We're all human, and I recognize that people are attracted by lurid headlines. And, of course, that's what the papers count on. Therefore, they'll do whatever they have to do to make the story fit the lurid title they've come up with. One of Hollywood's greatest stars was the subject of an article which blasted her for her arriving late at a charity benefit and refusing to be interviewed by the press. Readers were advised she acted as though she were "drunk." The true story was, the star was very ill and running a high fever. She'd been told by her doctors not to leave her bed, but she knew what her presence meant to the cause, so, despite the warnings, she got dressed and attended the gala. She could barely stand, let alone give interviews to the press. The press made their own decision, however, and an act of courage was turned into an exhibition of thoughtlessness. The paper made her sound like a self-indulgent witch. And that's how it's done—a truth is bent and twisted and embroidered until the actual reasons for what happened are buried.

Most stars let it go; they don't want to get embroiled in battles that create still more headlines. Some people fight back, though, and a few have won. In reality, of course, the victory is short-lived. Readers keep coming back.

Dad had attempted to meet the press onslaught head-on; he had hoped that, by speaking openly, he'd have some control over his own story. When he saw how the tabloids were treating him, he decided to try and fight fire with fire.

One of Dad's good friends was Johnny Carson. They'd known each other for years, and since both were mischievous at heart, they got along famously. Dad called Johnny Carson and asked him if he could be a guest on the "Tonight Show." Carson quickly said yes, and not just because he knew what a scoop it would be for his program. He had an idea what Dad was going through and was happy to have him use the "Tonight Show" as a forum.

Of course, the "Tonight Show" is booked way in advance. Since it was important for Dad to appear as soon as possible, the show's administrators did a little switching, and Dad was scheduled to appear two days later, on Thursday, May 9.

The next day, Dad's press representative released a story in *The Hollywood Reporter* saying Dad would be appearing on the "Tonight Show" to show people he wasn't "all that sick."

The release read in part, "He wants people to know he's hanging in there despite the deathbed stories appearing in the tabs. He wanted to go on a show and lighten up. It will not be maudlin. It will be fun."

Fun, yes, but there were many obstacles to Dad's goal, not the least of which was a rumor that a fee of fifty thousand dollars would be paid to any photographer who could get a shot of him at the taping. NBC responded accordingly and doubled the security to keep cameramen off the premises.

Even though Dad's appearance had been announced, the audience at the "Tonight Show" didn't know they'd be seeing him. Many ticket holders are out-of-towners who get their seats months in advance. As a result, most of them were astonished to see Dad in person.

The "Tonight Show" of May 9, 1991, attracted the second-largest audience in the program's last ten years. (In keeping with Dad's wry sense of humor, I have to tell you that his appearance with Johnny Carson was topped by the one on which Tiny Tim married Miss Vicky.) Once the studio audience knew Dad was going to be on the show, they began to buzz. There was a tremendous electricity in the air, all generated by Dad's upcoming appearance. The show opened and proceeded as usual. Carson did his opening monologue and the first commercials were aired. Then, seated at his desk, Johnny Carson faced the camera and began Dad's introduction.

"As you probably heard, Michael Landon recently announced that he had inoperable cancer of the pancreas and liver, and that would stun anybody. But, like Michael Landon, he met the problem head-on. He invited the press to his house and told them the situation. He did that mainly to avoid the rumors, the speculation, the misinformation, and to try to avoid sensationalism by the tabloids.

"And, for the past month, he has continued to face this battle with humor, honesty, and a personal sense of dignity that characterizes the man. Would you welcome Michael Landon."

Oh, and did that wonderful audience ever welcome Dad! They cheered and applauded as he stepped from behind the multi-hued curtain.

He took his place next to Johnny's desk and when the applause finally died down, the host began to talk. He told Dad it was good to see him and Dad replied that it was good to see *him*.

"I was really rather touched when you called and said you wanted to be on this show because I know every show in the country has been calling you to come on. I'm very flattered that you're here."

Dad spoke of his reasons for being on the show.

"The thing I want to clear up right away is the tenth-child business. There's a big headline in one of those incredible tabloid magazines about the fact that I want to have a tenth child so my wife will have something to remember me by.

"Here I've got nine kids, nine dogs, three grandkids—and one in the oven—three parrots, and my Cindy needs something to remember me by?"

The audience roared with laughter and Johnny Carson joined in. Dad had done it, he'd relaxed people, he'd made them laugh. Then he began to talk about his family.

"I love our life-style. With a houseful of kids you give each other strength. There are plenty of people who get a kick out of kids for, say, thirty minutes or an hour; I get a kick out of them permanently. It's such a pleasure to be with them, listen to them, watch them change, grow, become. Sure, they have quarrels, get ill, have accidents. It seemed we had only to put the car in gear and it headed down the hill to the emergency room. I had more stitches than any of them," laughed Dad.

"Once, I was giving little Leslie and Michael a soapy bath. I'd bathe them together; they'd escape. I'd chase. Well, once I slipped and went feet-first through a plate-glass window, cut a main artery, and blood spurted to the ceiling. Not to scare them, I just said, 'Get Mom, I need a tourniquet,' while these children wailed, 'Daddy, Daddy, are you going to die?'

"Well, I told them no, I was not going to die, and I didn't. I can't exactly promise them that now, but I can sure tell 'em we're going to fight."

Dad thanked everybody who'd gotten in touch with him and spoke about some of the suggestions people had offered, including one who suggested that if he swam with a dolphin, the sonar rays emitted by the leaping mammal would be transferred to him and would zap the cancer.

"What can I tell you?" quipped Dad. "Here I am going to all these hospitals and I only gotta go to Marineland!"

In general, Dad seemed intent on keeping the tone of the evening light. He and Johnny Carson relived some fun times together, told old stories, reminisced.

At the end of the show, Dad discussed the tabloids. He chided them for using gruesome headlines to describe his condition. He told the audience how Jennifer and Sean had been terrified by the dramatic, exploitative exclamations, especially the one which said, "It's Over." Dad had wanted to prepare the kids his own way, but the tabloids got there first. His children had learned about his condition from their little friends whose parents saw the stories. In his only display of irritation, Dad looked straight at the camera and called some of the tabloids the real "cancer in our society."

When the program ended, Dad smiled and waved good-bye. The audience rose to their feet and cheered him once again. And then he was gone. It was his last live appearance on the medium he had so enriched, and in which he had spent so much of his life.

Dad's appearance on the "Tonight Show" didn't alter the tabloids' approach to his illness, of course. Until he died, you could usually find some story promising to give the reader the inside dirt on the illness, complete with all the grisly details. You have no idea how low people can sink unless you're been caught up in a "big story" like this one, and have seen the tabloids in operation.

When Dad went in for his second CAT scan, a technician in the hospital actually made a copy of the scan and sold it to a paper. There wasn't anything photographers wouldn't do to catch a candid shot of him. Some of those last pictures of Dad leaving the hospital are so heartbreaking to see. And so unnecessary. Why would anyone want to see him that way?

Dad couldn't allow himself to be bothered by the press anymore. Once he'd had his say on the "Tonight Show," he put all his efforts into being with his family and settling his estate.

While he never actually gave up fighting, there was a perceptible change in his attitude when he heard the cancer had spread, and when he sensed that his body had begun to deteriorate. Despite his disagreement with the doctor who had prescribed it, he still gamely tried to follow a vegetarian regime and he kept up his reading. He seemed to have no enthusiasm for it, however; a resignation had set in. Even as he searched, he despaired.

Then he abandoned his nutritional regime, which he could no longer tolerate. I remember watching him stick his tongue out after those meals. He'd make a face and say, "I hate this stuff!"

Dad switched to the turkey and mashed potatoes with gravy which he loved. And that's what he told me he ate every day until he could no longer take solid foods.

I received a phone call one afternoon from my biological father's secretary saying that he was trying to reach me. I hadn't heard from him in a while and immediately returned the call.

My father explained that he'd phoned because he heard Dad had cancer. He was subdued and spoke kindly. He expressed his sadness at the awful turn of events and said at the end of our conversation, "You know, I really wanted to thank him for taking such good care of you."

I didn't know what to say. I'd been trying for so many years to get him to realize there was no contest between him and Dad. His need to be the solo father had damaged both of us. We both had lost because he set the stage with his win/lose rules and forced me to make choices.

That weekend when I went to see Dad, I told him what my father had said.

Dad looked at me for a long moment. We were both crying.

"It's about time," Dad whispered. "I hope he feels better saying it. It's about time."

Yes, it was about time. Unfortunately, time was running out.

★ ★ ★

The day Dad learned he had cancer, he began to change. In those final months of his life, the best of his natural instincts surged to the surface. His basic humility, his valiant spirit and loving soul, all returned. This was the dad I had longed to see again, the caring, loving, noble man of my childhood. What an awful price to pay, though, to regain the parent I loved, knowing he soon would be gone.

Our relationship in the past decade had grown strained; the reasons for the tension were obvious and valid and perhaps unavoidable. Dad had begun a new life for himself, and though he never turned his back on me completely, I had been relegated to the sidelines.

Ironically, though I was in the background, I stood by him. When he flew up to San Francisco to see me, we had been especially close. I had seen his anguish, his depression. I knew he was in turmoil. In a way, he was torn between his wants and his needs. He wanted to stay with Mom and us, but he needed to be with someone else. They say a want is not a need, so his final choice wasn't surprising. What he really needed was to face his personal problems rather than running away from them.

Once the decision had been made, a wall went up between us. And while there was a door in that wall that occasionally we could pass through to get to each other, most of the time the door remained closed.

As an adult, as a wife and mother myself, I was aware that the old relationship had to alter. You cannot go through life simply being your parent's child. You have to grow up. And yet you want to feel as though the parent is still part of your world. I got the feeling I was being pushed outside Dad's world, and not necessarily by him.

I needed him many times in those ten years. His guidance, his love, and his full support would have helped. He did provide some financial assistance on occasion, but as I've written, there was an underlying edge to his giving, a new and different attitude.

Had I not been in such a rocky situation, I doubt I would have noticed his distancing as much. I think I felt his reticence because I was going through such a bad time, being both sick and broke. I expected his support because he always had been there, every single time. I couldn't help remembering those times.

Once when I was working for the title insurance company in San Francisco, I'd come down to Los Angeles for a visit. Dad said, "Come on, beauty, let's go get an ice cream." I remember that we drove to the ice cream parlor and over our cones we talked about my future.

"I think it's great that you're working, Cheryl," Dad said, "but I can tell it's really important for you to be the teacher you want to be and go back to school. I've got so much money, baby, let me help you go back. I'll take care of it. You get an apartment and I'll pay for everything."

Dad always had anticipated my needs, offering to do things without my ever asking. After having known that kind of care and security, it was hard to accept his withdrawal.

Later, when I was so desperate, I felt ashamed of myself for being so needy. When I stepped back, I was able to see how everybody went to Dad for money, especially his new family. He had become the source for everyone's certainly better-than-average life-style. And while his paycheck had expanded and he could handle it, I, for one, opted to get out of the feed line. His generosity, once so spontaneous, now seemed an obligation. It was more important for me to have Dad's respect than his money.

While I temporarily lost a most significant person in my life, I was very fortunate to have found another.

At CEDU I had become acquainted with a staff member named Eddie. Eddie's mother, Mickey, had a master's degree in engineering and a Ph.D. in computer science. When Jim was looking for a career, I got in touch with Eddie and he suggested we see his mother. It sounded as if she'd be able to give us some good advice. Jim and I went to see Mickey Lutes, and that was the beginning of one of the strongest relationships in my life.

My friendship with "Momma Mick" coincided with the years of constraint between me and my dad, and her exceptional presence got me through that rough period. Like Dad, Momma Mick came from a humble background. She was a street-smart lady with a great heart. She became a mentor for me and Jim and guided us through difficult times. Momma Mick was sympathetic to a point, then she used "tough love." She "kicked me in the rump" and told me I had to get going on with my life. And she did this with such love, I had to respond. That blessed woman stood beside me when I desperately needed someone, and, more important, she understood how to help without making me totally dependent upon her. In that respect, she was wiser than Dad.

She believed in me and told me she'd help me get out of the pit if, and only *if*, I continued to work my hardest. I could do it because she gave me the necessary emotional support.

Momma Mick told me to keep a clear head and follow her instructions. She set up a financial reconstruction plan for Jim and me and we stuck to it. Meanwhile, because of several large, unpaid accounts, Jim and I had fallen behind in rent payments and the landlord served us an eviction notice. One night I was alone with my four-year-old son when a process server came to the house. I wouldn't let him in and he began pounding on the doors and windows. James Michael began to cry, and fortunately a neighbor came to our rescue. I couldn't believe this was happening.

During that time, I had done everything to avoid asking Dad for money. The landlord tried to force me to seek Dad's help by threatening to contact the tabloids and tell them Michael Landon's daughter couldn't pay her rent. I sold some of my jewelry, even some wedding presents, anything to keep us going.

We hung in and we got through, thanks to Momma Mick and our own unceasing efforts to become successful.

During that awful period when we saw so little of each other, I was learning another lesson from Dad, only it was being taught from the negative rather than the positive side. I was learning I could survive without him.

My brothers and sisters suffered, too. Dad made a big point for the press and for us that he didn't blame his children for being mad as hell at him for what he'd done. He told us to vent our anger as much as we wanted. When we calmed down, he reasoned, we'd realize he still cared for us. Dad wanted us around but we had to get rid of our negative feelings. He insisted upon a "love me, love my wife" attitude from his children.

Eventually, his psychology worked—to a greater extent on the younger kids. Once Mom and Dad were divorced, Dad's new wife became a kind of big sister to them. They could go over and have a great time at Dad's house, where they were wholeheartedly welcomed into the fold.

Dad was a proud and loving father. He not only gave his affection to James Michael, he wanted to do something for my son's future. Dad set up an educational trust fund for him and assured me and Jim that the fund would continue.

Dad became sad when he thought about missing the birth of Michael and Sherée's first child, Ashley, who was born a month after he died. Dad told a nurse that he had no doubt Michael would be a good father. He was amazed to see his own children have children of their own. "It gives one a sense of what 'forever' is all about," he said.

So I have to say, certain acts of generosity never stopped. Though Dad's everyday attention waned, his overall devotion remained as a steady undercurrent.

Because he was so distracted during the years after his remarriage, for the first time since Michael Landon had come into my life, I began to feel like an outsider.

When the cancer struck, however, everything fell away. I had no time to harbor any hurt feelings toward anyone, least of all my dad. I wanted to be with him and to help him in every way possible. I put aside these negative emotions and went to him with an open heart.

In May of 1991, I read the article Dad wrote for *Life* magazine. I had not known of his reaction to my automobile crash. He had made a promise to God in return for my life. He vowed to do something useful with his life and to make the world a little better because I recovered.

"Since that day," wrote Dad, "every script I've written and every series I've produced—not only 'Little House on the Prairie' and 'Highway to Heaven,' but the ones that didn't make it and the one I've just started—have expressed the things I most deeply believe. I believe in God, I believe in family, I believe in truth between people, I believe in the power of love. I believe that we really are created in God's image, that there is God in all of us."

I was overcome by the magnitude of what my dad was saying. He had asserted his faith in the Almighty and promised to serve him because of what happened to me! Here I'd always believed Dad was my inspiration, and now I learned, in a very significant way, I had been his.

25

*E*very weekend, Dad's children gathered at the house to be with him. All of us, including Mark and Josh, were in it together, and the only important thing was to rally behind him. We were not alone in wanting to bring about a miracle. Fans around the world were united by their love and admiration for their television hero; we were brought together by our love and devotion for our father.

Two fans began a campaign of hope. These incredible women collected and wrote messages of inspiration and pinned them to the gate of the Malibu house and all along the street. They hung purple ribbons on the trees and lampposts. They were never obtrusive. They went about their work quietly and efficiently and never disturbed our peace.

Peace? Well, maybe that isn't the word.

We did everything possible to lighten the burden for Dad. He was still the "big player," though, and was actively putting his estate together as he faced his illness and the specter of death. As much as we wanted to stand by him, in the final analysis, he was on his own.

Dad made rules. He didn't want a lot of crying, but on the other hand, he didn't want too much gaiety either. I guess this is fairly common among terminally ill people. They want the people around them to act normally, yet they don't want to see exaggerated cheerfulness. Perhaps it's too sharp a reminder of their own inability truly to enter in.

We were told we could visit with Dad on Saturdays and Sundays. When we came, we packed our own food in paper bags and brought it with us. We'd arrive and sit around in the kitchen or the family room. I can't help saying a word about Dad's new environment. He had left the Beverly Hills mansion for the "simple" life. Well, the simple life turned out to be pretty elaborate. The Malibu ranch had evolved into an extravagant multi-million-dollar palace.

At first, when Dad still had strength, he'd spend time with all of us. Even as he weakened, he insisted upon coming downstairs to the family room to receive us. He planned his blood transfusions around our visits. They gave him an added boost. If I close my eyes, I can still see him struggling to walk steadily as he picked his way across the room and eased his pain-racked body onto the couch. He would smile and say to one of us, "Come here, lovey, and sit next to me." What courage it took for him just to make that short trip across the room.

In June he really began slipping. His clothes hung on him. One of Dad's vanities had been his muscular build. He loved to wear T-shirts, which showed him off to greatest advantage. He was given tons of them and the first thing he did when he got them was to cut out the sleeves so that his well-developed upper arms were exposed. Maybe it was a way to erase the memory of his school days when he'd been forced to pad his clothing to make himself look bigger.

Now Dad stopped wearing the T-shirts. His arms, like the rest of him, were wasted.

While Dad was fighting the battle of his life, the young children would entertain themselves, or be entertained by their big brothers and sisters. One of their favorite games had Christopher dressing up like a pasty-faced Freddy Krueger and chasing his brothers, sisters, and nephew all over the lawn.

Dad got a big kick out of Chris's zombie-like makeup and told him he'd better watch out for photographers.

"They might get a shot of you and you'll find your picture on the front page of a tabloid with the headline, 'Stress Shows on Landon Children.' "

The contrast between the peals of laughter heard from outside the house and the fierce struggle going on inside was not lost on any of us. I know for a long while it was a comfort to Dad just to realize his children were out there, and that they would continue to be there, laughing and enjoying life, when he was gone. The laughter certainly was a great part of Dad's legacy.

Those last several weekends with Dad were some of the most healing times we ever spent together. We wanted more than anything to ease his pain and to see him through to the finish. We had been told by Cindy to come only on the weekend, Saturdays or Sundays, but Leslie, Michael, and I found it too constraining and began to come at other times as well, although I always had to fight the feeling that I was intruding. But, after all, my dad was dying, and why wouldn't I want to be by him as much as possible? Dad was more than glad to see me, and that made up for any discomfort I felt about going there, and we often broke his "no crying" rule.

Finding ways to entertain a dying person isn't easy. One thing we had going for us was Dad's invincible sense of humor. We created many diversions to amuse him and he loved every one of them. One of the first things I did was to write down all the "reactions" of the family and put them onto a sheet of paper for Dad to read. The collection was entitled "The Yenta Gazette by Muriel the Yenta."

Dad still referred to himself as the Jewish cowboy with all his goyim, and this goy made it her business to use the Yiddish words and sayings which Dad himself used and got such a kick out of.

I poked fun at everyone even as I was expressing our profound grief. Dad laughed and laughed at each entry of the Gazette. The jokes are personal and wouldn't mean anything to strangers, so there's no sense quoting them here. The main thing, however, is that I was writing for my dad again.

I made up poems and essays, just as I'd done when I was a little girl, and brought them to him. I wanted him to have tangible evidence of my absolute love. Every time I went to see him, I had something for him.

Besides my own writings, I brought books from the Course in Miracles I was taking. Dad was very interested in the inspirational works by Drs. Gerald Jampolsky and Bernard Siegel. When he was too ill to read, I read aloud to him. He really enjoyed them.

All of us together made up a special book of remembrance. Each child had a page filled with words and pictures in this homemade scrapbook of love. Dad pored over it. You could see him absorbing all the memories. He couldn't get enough. Neither could we.

One day, Michael and Leslie arranged for a plane to fly over the ranch trailing a banner which read "Us." We all went outside to watch the plane circling. At first, Dad got a kick out of it, but when the pilot continued to circle round-and-round he became nervous.

"Jesus Christ," exclaimed Dad, "this guy is so excited to be flying around my house, he's going to run out of gas and crash!" Dad ordered everyone to get back inside. Sure enough, the pilot flew off once his audience was gone.

During the time I was alone with Dad, he opened up and spoke of the past. He recognized that he'd gone through a period of mean-spiritedness and had been unduly nasty to people he really loved, not only us, but friends, even friends as close as Kent Mc-Cray. Kent and Susie came to visit him often. On one occasion, Dad was getting a blood transfusion and playing a hand of pinochle with Kent. Suddenly, Dad reached out, took Kent's hand and said, "I never really appreciated you enough. Thank you."

Dad fought like anything, and then finally accepted that he probably wasn't going to make it. It was agony, that last month and a half. I've watched four people die of cancer, including my granddaddy John. I remember my grandfather was undermedicated by his doctor and it made me furious that he wasn't given something more to dull the pain by his doctor.

The doctors were using experimental stuff on Dad, which may have caused him even more agony. I kept track of the medicines he was on. I wrote them down and noted the ways he was combining them. In addition, he used vitamins, enzymes, acupuncture, visualization and liposomes. Without warning, Dad could be affected. He'd be doing okay and then, suddenly, he'd be awash in perspiration, unable even to speak. He'd lift his head and look toward the window through which the sounds of the children's laughter could be heard. Then he'd start to hemorrhage, bringing up huge, horrible clots of blood. Dad didn't want us to witness these hideous attacks. He used all his strength to get through them and tried valiantly to act normal in front of us.

Dad often came up with witty comments on his situation. Because of his humor, we managed to have some laughs over his treatment, laughs he generated. Dad had to have many transfusions, and everyone who could donated blood. Mom recalls a story of how Bud Barish, who owned a Chrysler dealership, gave blood to Dad. When Dad was getting the transfusion, he was told whose fluid now coursed through his veins. "Oh no," said Dad mockingly. "Now I'll become a used car salesman."

Dad wanted to discuss current events. The Japanese work ethic was under considerable scrutiny at that moment, and comparisons were being made between their work forces and ours in America. Although Dad was one hundred percent for the U.S.A., he did think we could learn a lot from the Japanese, and he didn't like the idea of putting them down.

He talked of the things he enjoyed doing, especially travel. He had planned to go to the Galápagos Islands off the coast of Ecuador, a trip he had anticipated with great excitement. He urged us to go, to take the trip for him and see nature in its purest and most inspiring form.

He spoke of our early years together and told me again how proud he was of me for going against all odds and getting back those qualities he so loved in me. The old moxie!

A "death watch" becomes very blurred. The sadness and the sameness of the endless days merge, and even when you're actually going through it, there's a kind of mist over everything. Some details I recall vividly; others are much vaguer, and if I hadn't taken notes, I'm not sure I would believe they even happened at all.

Around the first of June, Dad began having severe anxiety attacks. He'd wake up several times during the night and become thoroughly frightened. He told the nurse he had two pressing fears. He was petrified of not being able to breathe and equally scared of dying in great pain. The nurse reassured him that he would not be in great pain because the doctors had inserted a morphine pump under his skin that would allow him to control the amount of painkiller. As for not being able to get air, the doctors felt Dad's breathing problems were emotional and told the nurse to treat any incidents with tranquilizers. They did seem to provide relief even when Dad was positively gasping for breath. Once the nurse found him sitting at the edge of the bed, holding on to his mattress for dear life and struggling for air so laboriously that the veins in his neck bulged. The nurse administered tranquilizers and the attack was over almost immediately.

By the second week in June, Dad was no longer going through the motions of keeping up appearances. He stayed in his pajamas all day; what was the sense of going through the strain of dressing? It took too much energy.

Dad told me he was seeing flashes of white lightning and hearing voices. That's when I accepted the fact that he wasn't going to make it.

Still, his mind was alert and fully engaged. He began to watch his old programs on television. "Bonanza" and "Little House" in the mornings and "Highway to Heaven" in the evenings.

"This is every actor's dream," he told the nurse, "seeing yourself on television from morning to night!"

By this time, Dad was hooked up to all the contraptions used to sustain life. And though he no longer bothered to dress, he remained adamant about concealing his suffering as much as possible.

More and more frequently, Dad would be overcome by nausea, and when that happened, he'd order everyone out of the room except for the nurse. He just didn't want the people he loved to see him suffer.

We all did special things for him. One day I brought my healing oils and asked if he wanted me to massage his feet.

"It'll make you feel better, Dad," I promised.

"Okay, beauty, you do it."

I took the oils and rubbed them around his legs and onto his feet. He was so weak he could barely move his legs on his own. I raised them as gently as I could. They seemed to be weightless.

"Oh, that feels so good," said Dad.

I looked up at his face. I was anointing my dad's feet with oil and this very act made me think of the time he had been at my feet calling me back to life. If only I could do that for him! But, of course, that was impossible; all I could do to ease his pain was to soothe his flesh.

We talked together while I used the healing oils. He told me about his love for his children and grandchildren. He spoke of his concerns about society and the world. As he spoke, I made a decision of my own. I had been wondering what I could do for him. I didn't know exactly what it would be, but I wrote and told him that, whatever else, I would honor and protect his name.

In the days that followed, I did anything I could to make him more comfortable, either in mind or spirit. Once in the supermarket I saw some glasses with candles in them and Hebrew writing on the side. I bought a dozen of them and the next time I went to see Dad, I put several around on his night table and lit them. Since I no longer could massage his feet because he was in such pain, I thought the soft glow of the candles would be a comfort. The light cast shadows on his face and form. Much later, I learned I had purchased "Yahrzeit" candles, Jewish memorial candles which are burned once a year in honor of the dead.

On Sunday, June 23, Dad said he was certain this would be his last week. "I've fought hard and now I'm weary to the bone," he said.

He got through the week, but he didn't think he would last the weekend. Because he was so sure he was near the end, he asked for all of his children to stay over at his home for the weekend of June 28.

"This will be the last time we'll all be together," he told his nurse. "The one thing I need to leave behind is good memories."

Dad confided a lot in Jim, the male nurse who attended him. Recently I talked with Jim and he told me how much he had grown to admire Dad. He spent many hours with him, "talking, laughing and delving into areas that one only speaks of when death is inevitable."

"No one," Jim said, ever "had the impact that your dad had on me." In fact, Jim no longer works directly with the terminally ill because, as he says, "it was the first time I ever lost a patient and a friend."

Shawna and Chris also had been a great comfort to him over the past weeks. Shawna was full of tricks and at one point started a water-pistol fight and even managed to target Dad. He loved it. Chris smuggled in a bag of candy, which Dad hid under the bed. Candy didn't come under the category of health food and technically was not allowed in his home. Dad said he wanted a candy bar, and Chris went and got two of every kind. Chris later went to Jack-in-the-Box to get Dad's last junk food request, a chicken sandwich.

There were also difficult and confusing times as each of us tried to deal with Dad's imminent death in our own way. Still, we shared the same bond—to love him as best as we could.

The disagreements of the past months were forgotten on that last weekend. All nine kids, various spouses and grandchildren came on Saturday. Dad had not been able to come downstairs to sit with us for some time. We went up to his room.

"No sad faces," he told us, "I don't want to see any sad faces." And so, on a long Saturday afternoon, we were together, surrounding him. In the early evening, Dad looked around at all of us and said, "This is as good as it gets."

The next morning, Jim the nurse felt the end wasn't far off and called us all upstairs. Again we gathered around the bed and talked in hushed tones. We thought Dad was in a coma.

"Didn't anyone ever tell you it's rude to whisper?" Dad admonished, and then fell back asleep.

At one point, he regained consciousness and looked down at the huge socks that were on his feet.

"I look like one of the Simpsons," he laughed.

Then he became serious.

"Is there anything you want to know?" he questioned. "Now is the time to ask."

"Is there anything you want us to do?" I asked.

"Just love one another," said my dad.

That evening we watched him struggle. He raised his fists and clawed at the air. I heard him mumbling, but I couldn't make out the words. He seemed to be running through various scenes in his life.

"No, not yet," he said clearly, "I'm not ready. No, I don't want to go."

The next morning we came up and stood around his bed. The nurse told us Dad had spent the night raising his hands and pawing at the air as though he was trying to keep something away.

Dad lay there with his eyes closed. Occasionally, he spoke. He wasn't talking to any of us, though, he was somewhere else. At one point I heard him say clearly, "Dad, you'll have to wait. I'll be with you in a minute. Oh, Mom, it's so pretty here."

Dad was so very, very weak, and still he struggled to live. It was awful to watch him, and we knew it had to end. It was time for us to say good-bye. One by one, we knelt next to his bed to say our farewells. I was one of the last.

I told him I could never say good-bye to him, and that he should not fight any longer. It was time to move on. Then I said, "Dad, it's time for you to go. Your ship is ready to set sail to the other side where loved ones are waiting for you."

"Yes," he said. "I've got to go."

Then Michael, Jr. said, "Dad, this is enough. It's time to move on."

His eyes still closed, he said softly, "You're right. It is time." Then he smiled and said, "I love you all."

Michael Landon died on the first of July, the very day on which his mother had been born.

26

Since Dad's body had to be removed privately, we were told not to inform the press or even to go outside the house. Nevertheless, we were later told that one of Cindy's relatives slipped out the door and went down to the gate where the reporters had gathered. He told one of them that Dad was gone and thereby set the wheels in motion for the havoc that followed. We were now at the mercy of the media, the very thing we had tried to avoid.

In a short while, all hell broke loose. The steady, metallic buzz of the press helicopter increased in volume as it dipped closer and closer to the ground. Television and movie sound trucks came roaring up to the front gate to join the forces already gathered there. We could hear the squeal of brakes as the cars came to a stop. We were protected by the security system, but the commotion outside our gates was frightening.

The funeral parlor was called and a car was sent to take the body away. We wanted to get Dad out of there without the photographers getting any pictures. We thought there might be cameras in the helicopter. One photographer managed to climb over the fence and began walking across the front lawn. The maid spotted him and told Jim. Jim ran out and tackled the intruder, pulling him to the ground. He grabbed the camera and threw it down hard. The camera flew open and the film was exposed. Jim was furious. He grabbed the cameraman and pulled him to his feet, then he hurled him down the lawn toward the gate.

"Get the hell out of here," he screamed.

The photographer ran like crazy to get away from Jim and scooted back over the fence. "Nobody's going to get a picture of Mike dead," said Jim when he walked back into the house. "Nobody." It was a promise he had made to Dad.

In order to get the body out, Jim and some of the others broke down the fence at the rear of the house. The hearse was backed out through the opening, and the reporters were kept away by my husband and Jim, the nurse, running alongside.

Armed guards were put on duty at the funeral parlor to make sure no one broke in.

Dad's private funeral service was conducted by a rabbi. Only family and close friends were present. Dodie, Dad's first wife, came with her sons. My mother didn't attend. She told each of us that she would go if we needed her, but not for herself. Later, I asked Mom why she'd stayed away.

"Cheryl, dear," she said, "I'm so sad for you and the other children. But for me, your dad's death occurred at the time of our divorce. I did my mourning ten years ago."

$$\boxed{27}$$

*I*n the prologue to this book I mentioned that my dad did something at the end of his life which shocked our family. I said I was filled with anger at what he'd done and had to work my way through that wrath before I could begin writing.

This is what happened.

During Dad's final illness, we were informed that he intended to write a personal letter to each of his children. He'd been so thoughtful in dealing with little Jennifer and Sean, we assumed he wanted to bid his older children an intimate farewell.

No letters were forthcoming. We were told he'd abandoned the idea. Furthermore, shortly after Dad had been diagnosed, he asked my brother Michael to get a video camera with ten tapes so he could record personal messages for each of us. We never received these, either.

Then we discovered that in the weeks prior to his death, Dad had changed his will. Without going into the details, I'll just say the new will adversely affected our family. Though each of the children from his prior marriages received a substantial sum, it was nowhere near what he'd originally indicated he had intended to leave us. Furthermore, he left no explanation as to why he suddenly altered his bequests. This was not characteristic of my dad.

I was deeply hurt when I heard the news. I was also upset to learn later that my son's educational trust would no longer be added to. Why this change after Dad expressly had told us it was a continuing fund? Dad knew the cost of education would escalate and had said he wanted to ensure James Michael's future by establishing a *growing* fund. Now I was told nothing more would be contributed. The whole business rocked me. I felt so helpless. I knew that if I raised questions, I would stand accused of being mercenary and risk losing any inheritance. To me, it wasn't characteristic of Dad to make such an extreme change without explanation.

Believe me, I hadn't been sitting around calculating what I was going to inherit; the only thing I had wanted was for my dad to live. But then I lost him, and immediately after that I was informed that he'd cut my inheritance. It seemed as though he had turned his back on me once again. What had I done wrong?

I talked to Momma Mick, who was dying of cancer herself. She comforted and advised me.

"Baby girl, no matter how coherent he seemed to be, your dad wasn't thinking straight at the end," said Momma Mick. "Listen, I know. I'm talking clearly to you and yet my mind is so mixed up from all the medicines I'm taking. And, baby, I'm not taking as much as your dad was.

"I know you think your dad was absolutely coherent. He wasn't. I'm telling you, he was in a fog. He had a lot of things on his mind. He could have been told to do anything, and he'd probably have done it. And, baby girl, face it, he had a new family."

Well, dear Momma Mick, I faced it. I accepted it. But only after I'd gone through the healing process at the retreat in Tiburon. What I learned there helped me to adjust, both to Dad's passing and to that sudden revision of his will, which I am certain will be explained someday.

What's done is done.

I cannot, I will not, measure Dad's worth in terms of money. Even if he'd cut me out without a penny, his legacy to me was incredibly rich. He had given me the best of what he had to give, and what he had was considerable. During the twenty years he watched over me, I received his unconditional love and guidance and finally at the end, his confirmed pride in me—that was his legacy. In the future, if I have moments of doubt, I'll remember those glorious years we shared. He saved my life, and moreover gave me the will to continue. Nothing could have been of greater value.

I wish I could have received a final letter or videotape from him, even if it had only been brief. Short of that, he did write, in his will, words I'll always hold in my heart.

"Although I could not legally adopt Cheryl," wrote my father, "she is my daughter."

Yes, I am Michael Landon's daughter, and with this book, I've kept my promise to my dad.

Postscript

I am writing this on the first anniversary of Dad's death. In the course of writing this book, I was forced to come to terms with a lot of emotions that had confused and upset me. I am still in the process of healing. There are so many unanswered questions that still haunt me.

I chose to write this book to keep my promise to Dad and to try and answer some of these questions. This has been one of the most difficult projects I have ever undertaken. My objective was to tell the story of Dad's life with the power of truth and love. Dad trusted me and was proud of me and it was this love that helped me write our book.

In the course of writing, there were facts I discovered which confirmed my trust in Dad's love for all of us, as his children. I was once again captured by the wonderful oneness I had felt as Dad's daughter, starting as the little girl and growing up in the shelter of his and Mom's love.

As I sought to understand more about his final days, I talked with the registered nurses who were with him constantly during the final months of his life. Dad revealed much to these professionals; they, in turn, shared his thoughts and statements with me. The nurses told me that as Dad was dying he spoke of his children. "I love my family, my kids more than anything. They mean the world to me," he said. One day Jim, the nurse, walked into a touching scene with my brother Christopher lying with his head on Dad's chest and Dad's arm around him. After Christopher left, it was time for the chemotherapy injection Dad had been putting off all morning. Dad's eyes welled up as he told the nurse, "God, I love these kids." The tears were running down his cheeks, the nurse described, as Dad desperately tried to regain his composure. Dad grabbed Jim's hand, he held it in his and apologized for losing control. "I don't know what I'm going to do without them, they're all I really have," he said.

Hearing what Dad said, knowing we were a constant in his thoughts, was comforting, but at the same time, what the nurses reported was troubling. We had felt obliged to follow certain courses of action based upon what we were told Dad desired. For instance, after he was told in mid-April that he only had three weeks to live, Cindy said Dad wanted us to continue our visits only on weekends, that he wanted to reserve his weekdays for her, their two children and Dad's doctors. Cindy said that he did not want to upset his regular routine. So we respected what we believed was "his" request and never questioned it. (How I cried so often at not being allowed to be with my dad other than those brief one-day weekly visits or an occasional visit here and there.) I learned from the nurses, however, that this wasn't really an accurate picture of what was going on during those final days. Dad thought we were too busy to come during the week and, characteristically, did not want to pressure us to spend time with him when there were other things we had to do. He wanted to see his children, *he even planned his transfusions and treatments around our weekend visits*, yet he didn't want to upset our routines. Obviously, this was not the option presented to us. Not wanting to see us is quite different from not wanting to bother us. Had I known how he really felt, I'd have given up anything to be at his side from the beginning to the end, just as he had been there for me after my accident. And, sadly, though the week days were reserved for Cindy and Dad's doctors, the nurses' records show that Dad was often left alone for long periods of time, with only a nurse as company. Whatever the reasons, I deeply regret the loss of those precious moments with him, and I'm deeply saddened that he might have misunderstood why we weren't there.

It also saddens me to think Dad felt an urgent need to make major changes to his will, especially when he was so terribly ill. It still hurts that there was no explanation from Dad. As one of the nurses said, "It's unthinkable that the father of all fathers would do this to his children. That isn't the Michael Landon I knew."

I have read recently of Cindy's concern that I might say something in this book that Dad wouldn't have liked. I am sorry she feels this way as I have said nothing that would upset my dad. The truth is, however, that she and I did not know the same man, and certainly did not know him in the same way. The man I know raised me as his daughter for thirty years, and our relationship was naturally different. I do believe both Cindy and I shared how Dad lifted us out of loneliness and despair and gave us a solid home. The man I know embraced us and warmed us with his love and generosity. He directed me to be honest and I have felt his guiding hand throughout this project.

Looking back, I recalled the car crash twenty years ago and the second chance I was given to make use of my life. I later learned Dad had made his promise to God in return for my survival. Little did I know at the time that I would make a promise to my dad, and would be forced to surrender him to the same God that gave me back my life.

The years of growing up with Dad were some of the most magnificent years of my life. After Dad left us, he had undergone a change, some of it due to his growing older, some of it brought on by the inescapable pressures of life in the celebrity "fishbowl," and some to a growing, silent depression. Even so, through it all, Dad continued his wonderful work bringing light to darkness, and was an inspiration to us all.

Michael Landon is my hero as well as my dad, and heroes must not be forgotten. Dad is an angel of light who was human and my mother the gracious lady who stood beside him and gave him strength. I believe we must keep Dad's visions alive, his teachings flourishing, and remember him with the smiles and laughter he so deserves.

Through all the years, one thing has never changed—the love and respect I feel for him remain to this day, a part of my soul. Though I am still grieving, healing and continuing my search for answers, our love is eternal.

I remain a very spiritual person. Like Dad, I believe in God and the oneness of mankind. And, as my dad taught me, I believe in the power of love and in the ability of any individual to use that love to communicate with another. I believe that love is a legacy, the greatest gift one person can give to another. That was the gift Michael Landon gave to me. He is one of the greatest inspirations in my life.

I have mentioned several times how Dad encouraged me to write, to find ways to express myself. At the end, when he knew his time was so short, I wrote a poem for him. It is called "A Song of Love for You," and I read it to him at the same time I gave him a collage of photos of the years we had shared. He looked at these pictures, remembering, I know, all the happiness of that earlier part of his life. And he smiled with pride and tenderness at the words I read him. The poem is long and personal, but I do want to share the last few lines because they speak of my love for this man, and of my prayer for his regained happiness.

Just one more time
Let us look into your eyes
And show you how much we love you.
How much we will miss you!

Our song of love will protect you on your journey . . .
It will keep us together as we go our way.

Let us sing our song with powerful voices,
Hopeful and strong.
Even if this is our last time to be together . . .
For now . . .

   Until we meet again.

        This song of love is for you!

I can never say goodbye to you . . .

Dearest Dad, I'll love you forever.

Dad triumphed with wonderful family programs and we must continue with Dad's inspirational messages. Let us begin at home with ourselves, our loved ones, and use this power of love to make our world safe for all to prosper. Let us work together to make it happen.

Acknowledgments

Thanks to the family, friends and associates of Michael Landon and Cheryl Wilson, who gave generously of their time.

Many thanks to Amy Appleton and Sidney Sheldon Welton for their insightful observations and suggestions, to Paul Mahon for his astute and helpful comments, and to Ila Gross and the LEAP organization.

Special thanks to Susan Ginsberg, wise agent and good friend.

My gratitude and thanks to Chuck Adams, editor and friend, and to Alice Mayhew who immediately recognized a good story.

Finally, I learned to admire and respect Michael Landon through his daughter Cheryl Landon Wilson. No father could wish for a more loving, just, and worthy child.

J.S.

I want to acknowledge Brenda Kimball for her sixth sight in creating this book and her sisterhood; Carolyn Kennedy, my personal assistant and dear friend: "I'm so proud!"; Chuck Adams, the most unusual editor who had a great sense to trust his feelings and "grab" a story; Alice Mayhew, a very special woman and the double to my beloved "Momma Mick," to whom I offer gracious gratitude; and "Lady" Jane Scovell, an unusual writer and special family to me.

Also my agent/attorney, Paul Mahon, everybody's dream of an agent and friend "I told you so!"; Marjorie Margoles, my other agent, here's to your success as congresswoman!; Helene Branch, let the dream live on!; my business associates, Ron Speakman, Arnold Gold, Bill Liebman, The Laconos, Vicki and Tom Merkens, Dennis/Copy King, Westlake Photo Lab, MGM Grand Airlines, Lily and Eileen. Also Janet and her sister for promoting love and hope through their purple ribbons, and DaValentino for the best pizza and cappuccino in New York.

Also my "healing team": Dr. Rashid Khan, without whom this book would not have been possible, the Arizona Department of Public Safety of Tucson, the St. Mary's Hospital emergency team, the cleaning lady, and Jane Sheldon's medals. I'd also like to acknowledge my other "rescuers," Uncle Bob, Joyce Blair, Susie Sitar, neighbor Tracy North, Dennis Brent, Scott Bailey, Nooner, Jessica Mosie and David Miller. Also Diane and Dr. Gerry Jampolsky, who taught me how to get out of the darkness and into the light, and their staff of angels at the Center of Attitudinal Healing in Tiburon, California, with Dr. Tom Pinkson and Zolinda as my mentors. Also Drs. W. Deardorff and M. Sinel, Barb and Frank, Jeannie Fournier, Pat Brown, Dr. Lori Phillips, Doreen, Becky, Valois, SCOI Medical Group, Callan Pickney's Callanetics and Polly St. John. Also my special family at Cedu and Cascade including favorites Eric, Mark and the Wasserman family. Also Susie and Jim Moore, friends one can always count on!

A special thanks to all the teachers of the world, most significantly Mother

Teresa, Marianne Williamson, Dr. Bernie Siegel, Dr. Brian Weiss, John Brad-
shaw, Robert Dilts and Anthony Robbins who have directly affected our lives
with their work.

Thanks to Susie and Kent McCray, who were my anchors after Dad's
departure; to Dad's crew and cast with special fondness to Ruth, Evie and
Harry Flinn. To Jay Eller, one of the very first who supported me in doing this
book, thank you for your trust in me to honor Dad, and to your staff. To my
other families, Susie, Bob and Colby Noe, and Virginia Noe, my Ginny Jean,
along with Lynwood Kern, my Aunt Woo, the greatest of Southern belles and
incredible ladies! I am so lucky to have "you all" in my life as relatives and
close friends. The Lipskys, everyone should have a Marilyn (as a devoted
friend you can depend on with nurturing love) and a Jay in their family. I am
so blessed! To my Italian family, I have learned through healing my child
within; I am free and able to enjoy you all. I am proud of my heritage! We are
so very passionate. A special passion always remains with my other sister,
Beth, and brother, Adam. To the Wilson families, fine people demonstrating
true Canadian charm with warmhearted spirits.

Thanks to family friends: Eleanor and Ray Moscatel, Dorothy and Bud
Barish, Mike North, Olive Stern, and Lois Snipenger, who made a great
difference with this book! Thanks to my friends, you all know who you are!
To all my Delta Gamma sisters and Susan Marx for encouraging me.

Thanks to Dad's registered nurses and medical team for going above and
beyond their call of duty! With special thanks to Lisa and Jim for their love
honoring Dad.

To role models, Jacqueline Kennedy Onassis, Barbara Walters, Oprah Win-
frey, Gloria Steinem, Gloria Estefan, Shelley Duvall, Penny Marshall, LA-
DIES Group and MADD. Thanks to Dr. Reverend Jesse Jackson, Edward
James Olmos and Jim Brown, some fine angels behind the Los Angeles
Rage. . . . Let's work together to heal this once city of The Angels.

In memory of Jim Henson for helping us to discover the child within us . . .
to Barbra Streisand, who showed us the need to heal that child within . . . to
Oliver Stone, for his courage to promote the importance of democratic film
expression.

In loving memory of General John, Bill and Foster Noe, Art Kern, "Ma
Cartwright," Momma Mick, Mom Alice and Earl, Poppa, Dan Blocker, Victor French, "Teddy," Lee North, Stuart Jason Siegel, Deni Danielle Ya-
coobian, Cathy Stubbins, Dennis and Mike.

In honor of our great leaders who sacrificed their lives for our freedom:
President Abraham Lincoln, Martin Luther King, Robert and President John
Kennedy: "I look forward to an America which will not be afraid of grace and
beauty."—JFK, 1963.

To all my Landon loves, without whom my life is incomplete. Dad left
behind many extensions of himself (with his lady's help)—including my sisters
and brothers, their spouses, and their children: Leslie, one of the child psy-
chologists, who truly knows the spirit of the child within and the purity of a

natural soul with Dad's sense of humor! I have been fortunate to have a sister who is also a dear friend. She symbolizes one of the first truly romantic times in Mom and Dad's life. Michael Jr.: I have told him for years he is a future Steven Spielberg with Dad's natural ability to inspire using his own style, and a great sense of humor! He's a brother I honor as my friend; he brings pride to us all. Shawna, I see the childlike spirit of Dad with a generous heart and creative flair whom I so cherish and will protect with my love as she spreads her wings and learns to fly. Christopher, truly a gift of love to us all! Another filmmaker in the works with a unique sensitivity, who is great fun to "cut loose" with and the last to be created from Mom and Dad, forming our "Landon Dream." Mark and Josh so touched are we by Dad's adoption as his children! There remains a special bond to these brothers that I honor and love. Jennifer and Sean, Jennifer already a talented actress with an adoring heart; and Sean, a specially bonded friend and "uncle" to my son, James-Michael. I respect both as my sister and brother and love them very much. Dad was proud of Cindy's maternal abilities. I agree because she is a great mother to them. To my sisters-in-law Sharee and Brenda, with Brian, my brother-in-law and their families: Thank you for making such a delightful difference in our lives.

To Dad's grandchildren, James-Michael, Monica and Danielle, how he delighted in their sweet innocence and peals of laughter . . . and to Ashley, our newest little angel and grandchild, though Dad missed seeing her arrival, I believe he witnessed her birth from above with tears of joy. All these extensions greatly touch our lives as they continue Dad's legacy described by him as: "It gives you a sense of what forever is all about." The idea that he would live on through his children, grandchildren, and great-grandchildren pleased him enormously. "Love is what lets you live on, it's the most powerful thing in the universe. Don't ever take it for granted." (Quoted from nurse's journal)

To Jim Wilson, my knight and dear companion. Thank you for your love and support in allowing me the time and space I have needed to complete this book and to move forward with my life. To quote Dad directly, "I'm proud you're part of my family." To the greatest treasure of my life, our son, James-Michael . . . my inspiration to go on against all odds.

Thank you to all the Michael Landon fans who continue to keep Dad's memory alive. I would like to acknowledge my mother, my father, Dad and our Heavenly Father. Without them I would not be here! Lastly, to anyone I missed—you will be remembered in Book 2: *The Healing While Writing This Book*.

Let's honor Dad's last request to "Love one another!"

C.L.W.